W9-CFJ-281

Alex McFarland

The 10 Most Common Objections to Christianity

Regal

From Gospel Light
Ventura, California, U.S.A.

PUBLISHED BY REGAL BOOKS
FROM GOSPEL LIGHT
VENTURA, CALIFORNIA, U.S.A.
PRINTED IN THE U.S.A.

Regal Books is a ministry of Gospel Light, a Christian publisher dedicated to serving
the local church. We believe God's vision for Gospel Light is to provide church leaders
with biblical, user-friendly materials that will help them evangelize, disciple and minister to children, youth and families.

It is our prayer that this Regal book will help you discover biblical truth for your own life
and help you meet the needs of others. May God richly bless you.

*For a free catalog of resources from Regal Books/Gospel Light, please call your Christian supplier or
contact us at* 1-800-4-GOSPEL *or* www.regalbooks.com.

Library of Congress Cataloging-in-Publication Data
McFarland, Alex, 1964-
   The 10 most common objections to Christianity / Alex McFarland.
      p. cm.
   ISBN 0-8307-4298-0 (trade paper)
   1. Apologetics. I. Title.
   BT1103.M335 2007
   239—dc22

                                                                          2006039488

1 2 3 4 5 6 7 8 9 10 / 10 09 08 07

Rights for publishing this book in other languages are contracted by Gospel Light Worldwide, the international nonprofit ministry of Gospel Light. Gospel Light Worldwide
also provides publishing and technical assistance to international publishers dedicated
to producing Sunday School and Vacation Bible School curricula and books in the languages of the world. For additional information, visit www.gospellightworldwide.org;
write to Gospel Light Worldwide, P.O. Box 3875, Ventura, CA 93006; or send an e-mail
to info@gospellightworldwide.org.

With love, prayers and much appreciation,
this book is dedicated to:

Marianne K. Hering,
Tom Neven
and
Focus on the Family's
Teen Ministries staff

Contents

ACKNOWLEDGMENTS

The following people have not only helped to make this book a reality but have also shaped my life deeply.

Special thanks are due to the wonderful team that makes up Gospel Light/Regal Publishing. This includes Bill Greig III, Alex Field, Mark Weising, Kim Bangs, Josh Talbot, Rob Williams and Marlene Baer, to name but a few. Theological editor Bayard Taylor also deserves special mention for his insights and assistance. I thank the Lord for each of you.

To Warren Smith, a gifted journalist, brother and friend, who helped me format and clarify this work. His editorial help was vitally important in the final stages of this book. I am grateful for your help.

Deepest appreciation goes out to Norman Geisler, Ph.D., whose books on apologetics changed the trajectory of my life from 1985 through today. Thanks also go out to the dynamic faculty, staff and students of the institution he founded—Southern Evangelical Seminary and the Veritas Graduate School of Apologetics. When Dr. Geisler and the Board of SES/Veritas asked me to become president, my wife and I were welcomed with open arms. Special appreciation is also due to Mrs. Barbara Geisler, Bob and Lynn Westra, and to Christina Woodside. What a help and blessing you all are!

Special thanks are due to several friends who have mentored me and who have given continual encouragement and inspiration. These include: Lee Strobel, who graciously took time to write the foreword; Mark Mittelberg, who is a role model in the area of apologetics-based evangelism; Gary R. Habermas, Ph.D., who, besides being an expert on the resurrection of Christ, is a role model, friend and continual encourager; Mike Licona, whose head for truth is matched only by his great heart for people; Jon Robberson and the staff of Spirit West Coast—it is such an honor to be a part of the work you do for Christ; the bold, brilliant staff of Wheatstone Academy and their leader, Brian Nick; John Mark Reynolds, Ph.D., of Biola University (if Edison had not invented the light bulb, not to worry, John Mark Reynolds would have provided illumination enough); and Dr. Harold Willmington, who is the personification of what it means to know, love and live the Bible. Finally, I extend heartfelt thanks to my former professor and Sunday School teacher, Dr. Elmer Towns, who graciously recommended me to Bill Grieg III and Gospel Light/Regal.

Very, very special thanks are due my wife, Angie. Angie does much for the Savior and for me, her spouse. She made many contributions to the completion of this book and also to my betterment. Finally, I am thankful for the Bible, which for 20 years has been an ever-present friend. Most of all, I am grateful for the Lord Jesus Christ, who loved me and gave Himself for me.

FOREWORD

I'm a skeptic by nature, which probably explains why I studied journalism and law and worked as a reporter and legal editor at *The Chicago Tribune*. At a young age, my skepticism drove me to atheism. Even though I had never taken the time to thoroughly examine the evidence, I figured it was ridiculous to believe in an all-loving, all-powerful Creator. My opinion was that God didn't create people, but that people created God out of their own fear of death.

My agnostic wife's conversion to Christianity, and the subsequent positive changes in her character and values, prompted me to embark on a serious investigation of the claims of Christianity. All kinds of questions blocked my path: Does the Bible stand up to scrutiny? Doesn't evolution disprove the need for a Creator? Aren't Christians arrogant when they say Jesus is the only ticket to heaven? What about the issues of evil and hell, and the hypocrisy I saw all too often among Christians? These are legitimate questions that deserve thoughtful and insightful responses. And that's what my friend Alex McFarland provides in this excellent new resource.

I've grown to trust Alex as a smart, passionate and persuasive defender of Christianity. His life's mission is to help spiritual seekers find satisfying answers to the sticking points that are holding up their journey toward God. Alex's mission is also to help Christians better communicate the evidence for their faith to their friends, neighbors, colleagues and family members. So whether you're investigating Christianity for the first time or whether you're a Christian who's wondering how to respond to objections your skeptical friends raise, you're going to get a lot of helpful guidance in Alex's new book.

As for me, I tried to keep an open mind as I studied everything from cosmology and genetics to archaeology and ancient history. My personal conclusion was that a raft of discoveries in half a dozen scientific disciplines over the past 50 years point powerfully toward the existence of a Creator. And I also found that there are convincing historical reasons for believing that the New Testament accurately depicts Jesus of Nazareth as the unique Son of God who proved His divinity by rising from the dead. Based on the evidence, I became a follower of Jesus—and ever since then I've been on the most incredible and fulfilling adventure of my life.

Who knows what awaits you? Begin the adventure now by turning the page and considering the factual foundation that undergirds Christianity. I hope you'll decide at the outset to go wherever the evidence takes you—even if it's to the astounding conclusion that Jesus is who He claimed to be.

Lee Strobel
Author, *The Case for a Creator* and *The Case for Christ*
www.leestrobel.com

A Clue for Those in the Search

I was in jail a few years ago. The Guilford County Jail, about 70 miles north of Charlotte, North Carolina. A mere block from where the infamous 1979 Nazi-Klan shootout left a trail of blood.

Okay, so I wasn't exactly the one being incarcerated. I was preaching there on an icy Saturday morning to a hallway packed with prisoners. Some were leaning against the inside metal of their cell blocks, others were given permission to venture into the common area. Some were sitting on chairs or the floor; others were standing in the back. But all of them, on that memorable morning, were captivated by the words of a young preacher.

After a sermon and a brief Q&A session, I asked if anyone would like to pray with me to ask Jesus into their life. To my amazement, virtually every hand went up. I prayed with them and afterward shook hands with most of the guys. But as I was meeting the inmates, I noticed a guy standing off in the back, eyes darting from me to the floor, me to the floor. I knew he had something to say.

"Preacher, I wanna know something," he said nervously after finally approaching me. "How good do you think a man has to be to get to heaven?"

His eyes told the story. This was his last hope.

"How do you think somebody can know if they gonna go to heaven when they die?" he asked again.

"What I think doesn't matter," I responded. "But I will tell you what the Bible says about it."

"How good is good enough?" he asked.

"Well, getting into heaven has nothing to do with being good."

A puzzled look came over his face.

"The Bible says in order to go to heaven you have to be *righteous*. Righteousness is like absolute purity, sinless perfection . . . you know, holiness. To get into heaven, you've got to be more than good; you've got to be as holy as Jesus. That's righteousness, and the Bible says that righteousness is God's litmus test for anyone getting into heaven."

"Oh . . ." he said, trailing off with a look of utter hopelessness.

"Yeah, 'oh' is right!" I said. I began to explain that the Bible's assessment of humans is that we are sinners. That God's standard is righteousness, but we aren't righteous. We don't have "righteousness," and we can't earn it. So God gives it, as a gift, for all who will receive Christ in faith.

As my words hit home for the inmate, there was a shift in his demeanor. He wanted to be ready for life after death. After praying to welcome Christ into his life, his entire appearance changed. A huge weight had been lifted off his shoulders. He could breathe again.

Why the dramatic change? Why the sudden life-altering turnaround from hopelessness to confidence? It was all because of an explanation—a reason to believe. This man needed someone to help explain the truth to him, not just another flimsy notion. And all it took was a few words.

Enter at Your Own Risk

You may have picked up this book for one of several reasons. Maybe you, like the prisoner I met, just need a few words to help you along the way. Maybe you frequently find yourself in heated conversations with non-Christians, struggling to defend your faith, and you're hoping this book might give you some ammo for your next battle of the wits. Maybe you're unsure of what you believe and are simply checking out some reasons why this Jesus thing may be the real deal. Or maybe you're an unwavering atheist interested in seeing how ridiculous the arguments are on the "other side."

Whatever your reason for picking up this book, I need to warn you of something before you dive in:

This book could be fatal.

I'm not trying to sound melodramatic, nor am I trying to inflate this book's importance. But in essence, this book deals directly with matters of the soul, and it's essential that you check your motive before going any farther. We'll be addressing some of the core issues involved with believing in God and what it means to be a Christian. And anytime you deal with those issues, you're dealing with God Himself—and our profound ability to either accept Him or reject Him.

If you find it hard to believe that there even is a God and if your motive is to honestly seek intellectual reasons that may reveal His existence, great. Hopefully this book can challenge both your mind and your heart. If you're full of questions about who God is and how to make sense of Him in a world that seems so opposite to who He says He is, even better. Questions are welcomed. Trust me; God's big enough to handle your queries. He's not intimidated by the depth of your scrutiny.

But, if you're out to disprove God; if your purpose for reading this book is simply to bolster your defenses against Him; if you're determined that no truth will ever be enough; if you're sitting at the intellectual chess table thinking you've got God cornered and are daring Him to a match . . . be warned. Truth be told, you'll probably be worse off after having read this book.

Why so dramatic? you ask. Because this isn't just mental gymnastics here. I'm all for intellectual sparring. I love to sharpen my mind with the best of 'em. But, simply put, this book could very well either lead to your salvation or seal your damnation. It's choose-your-own-adventure time. We're not just dealing with brainpower here . . . we're handling the soul.

Hello, My Name Is Alex

There's a fascinating element that comes into play whenever you deal with God. You see, He's the great connector of the mind *and* heart. With one stroke, He can woo you with both the most profound thought *and* the most penetrating emotion.

That's exactly what happened to me. I was raised in church most of my early life. In fact, I went to one of the oldest, most historic churches in my home state of North Carolina. Like generations of McFarlands before me, I attended Buffalo Presbyterian Church in Greensboro—a church that's now 250 years old. (Impressive, huh?) There I learned a lot about God, the Bible, Jesus and Christianity. But it wasn't until college in the mid-1980s that I entered into a personal relationship with Jesus Christ.

I was invited to a Monday night Bible study group held at a nearby church. I didn't want to go, but a girl I was interested in would be there, so I decided to show up. Actually, it felt pointless to listen to some guy talking about the Bible for an hour. What else did I need to know? After all, *my* church was on the national registry of historic places. (Have I mentioned how old my church was?) I'd been religious all of my life. What could some no-name, blue-collar church *really* offer an uptown guy like me?

Like the apostle Paul, I had a Damascus road experience. It wasn't until the third time I went to this Bible study, but it nonetheless did a number on me. Sure, I'd known *about* God. I had a ton of facts stored in my head for anytime someone wanted to talk "religion"—and I even believed the facts I had memorized. But prior to that summer of 1985, I'd never had a personal relationship with Jesus.

That all changed. And drastically! After asking Jesus to be Lord of my life, I couldn't worship enough, couldn't get enough of the Bible and couldn't talk about Jesus enough. In fact, I couldn't stop talking about Him with everyone I knew. Only two days after coming to a personal faith, I went with another college buddy to talk with a crowd of people who had congregated in a local park. It was the off-campus hangout place where students went to drink and party. My friend was also a new Christian, and he and I wanted to share the gospel with the university students who hung out there.

I'll never forget the scene: Three guys were sitting around a picnic table, passing around a joint. My friend and I were stumbling along, trying to persuade these guys that they needed Christ to forgive their sin. "See what I mean?" my friend said. "That beer and pot you've got there, that's a sin. Only Jesus can forgive sin!"

That didn't go over so well.

"I'm a philosophy major, and I don't believe there is a God," said one student. Another one of the guys passed the hash on and looked directly at me. "My anthropology professor said that Jesus Christ never existed. How am I supposed to believe in some guy who never really existed?"

My friend and I were stuck. There was an awkward silence as we exchanged glances. From the picnic table a third guy said, "Okay, we talked about this in my ethics class. Morals, rules, sin, whatever, man . . . it's different for different cultures. Right, wrong, good, bad . . . it's pretty much all the same."

The two other students looked back and forth from their friend to us, waiting to hear who would respond first. "Sin is a concept that religious people developed in order to control others," the guy added.

I had to say *something*. "Guys, I know there's an answer. I don't have the answer to all of these questions right now, so I'll get back with you on it. But I'll tell you this: The gospel is real, and you all need Jesus!" As we walked away, I felt completely defeated. In fact, I felt like I owed the guys an apology. So I went back, paused and stammered, "I'm sorry that I wasn't really prepared to tell you what I came to tell you."

They laughed as I walked away a second time.

You're the Inspiration

More than failing these guys, I felt like I'd failed God. I'd blown my chance to share His good news. Dejected at home that night, I thumbed through my Bible. I came across a verse I'd never seen before—one that was about to set the course for the rest of my life. It was 1 Peter 3:15: "But in your hearts set apart Christ as Lord. Always be prepared to give an answer to everyone who asks you to give the reason for the hope that you have" (*NIV*).

The next day I made a trip to my local Christian bookstore, having never set foot in one before. "Are there any books about how to answer questions that people have about God or the Bible?" I promptly asked the man at the counter. "You know, any books about even *objections* people have against Christianity?"

If there was ever a moment of divine providence in my life, this was it. "Oh, you're talking about *apologetics*," the man answered. He led me over to a shelf of books by authors whose names I had never heard of: C. S. Lewis, Francis Schaeffer, Chuck Colson. For a 21-year-old who was only three days into the faith, these authors looked pretty complicated.

The books that appealed to me most were by some guy named Josh McDowell. He'd written two volumes of *Evidence That Demands a Verdict*, so I bought both. They read like a legal deposition and were every bit as complex as the other books, but somehow I was drawn to these "quotation-heavy" volumes. I also bought his *More Than a Carpenter*, which I read and reread until it was literally falling apart. Within six months, I had bought several dozen apologetics books and was visiting the New Horizons Christian Bookstore every other week, burying myself in the works of guys like A. B. Bruce, B. B. Warfield, Charles Hodge, James Orr, C. S. Lewis and G. K. Chesterton. Within a year I'd ordered and purchased more than 100 books. More important, I was gaining the tools to explain my beliefs to other students on campus.

I eventually transferred to Liberty University in Lynchburg, Virginia, where I earned a master's degree in Christian Thought/Apologetics under one of the most influential figures in modern-day Christian apologetics, Dr. Norman Geisler. After writing a piece in the local newspaper about Christmas, churches began to invite me to speak about apologetics. By 1996, I was on the road full-time as an apologetics speaker, explaining the Christian faith in 50 states, more than 400 different churches, on 100 college campuses, in 27 major prisons, and in dozens of Christian schools.

Everybody's Got a Question

It's those travels—or more precisely, the people I met through those travels—that led me to write this book. In the past decade, I've sensed a greater need for Christians to be able to defend their faith. Believers have questions about their faith—lots of them—but it seems as though many don't know where to turn for answers. To me, that's where the power of apologetics comes in: to evangelize the lost and educate the saved.

Every honest question deserves a good answer. Don't you hate it when someone responds to your heartfelt question with a scripted, plastic pat answer? Instead, a good apologetics response to someone's question should be biblically accurate, factually correct and existentially satisfying. In other words, for both general and specific issues, our apologetics considerations need to be theological, reasonable and practical.

- Theological—Does what I say square up with the Bible?
- Reasonable—Does what I say make sense? Is it credible and factually correct?
- Practical—Am I giving people truth that is relevant to life? Have I successfully bridged the gap from the "ivory towers of academia" to the "real world" where people live their day-to-day lives?

I pray that this book is all three of those things. It is by no means the ultimate authoritative source on all things Christian, nor does it answer every question you might have about your faith. These are simply the 10 most common questions I've encountered as I've dialogued with thousands of people of all ages across all 50 states. The answers I've come up with have come to me through intense Bible study, reading the works of great Christian thinkers past and present, and lots of prayer. Some might be shorter than you'd like. The truth is, each of these questions could be a book unto itself. But my goal isn't to just load you up with head knowledge, as much as I appreciate that. Rather, I pray that this book offers you the perfect blend of intellectual reasoning and spirit-led faith—all for one purpose: to know Jesus and to make Him known!

The Questions of Life

In sepulchral black and red, the cover of Time magazine dated April 8, 1966—Good Friday—introduced millions of readers to existential anguish with the question, Is God Dead? If he was, the likely culprit was science, whose triumph was deemed so complete that "what cannot be known [by scientific methods] seems uninteresting, unreal." Nobody would write such an article now, in an era of round-the-clock televangelism and official presidential displays of Christian piety . . . What was dying in 1966 was a well-meaning but arid theology born of rationalism: a wavering trumpet call for ethical behavior, a search for meaning in a letter to the editor in favor of civil rights. What would be born in its stead, in a cycle of renewal that has played itself out many times since the Temple of Solomon, was a passion for an immediate, transcendent experience of God.

JERRY ADLER, JOURNALIST[1]

We live in an odd time. You know that something doesn't add up when a mere click of the television remote separates Pat Robertson, Howard Stern, SpongeBob SquarePants and South Park (now on network TV, of course). In our post-Nipplegate world, secular and nonsecular critics alike note a decline in our nation's morals. In contrast, while conservative activist groups and concerned parents are protesting louder than ever, Internet pornography continues to expand to a multi*billion* dollar business and audiences faithfully flock to the latest $100 million-earning sex comedy or horror flick.

Philosophers have dubbed our era a postmodern one in which relativism reigns supreme. *Whatever works for you, man. Whatever floats your boat.* This explains the moral dichotomies that are in action. As Ralph Waldo Emerson once said, "Consistency is the hobgoblin of little minds." With this statement, Emerson, one of the intellectual fathers of modernism, dismissed out of hand the need for ideas to be logically compatible. And that allowed, to a degree, the rise in spiritualism or, as Jerry Adler calls it, the "era of round-the-clock televangelism."

Almost 80 percent of all Americans describe themselves as "spiritual." The same number believes that God created the universe. Two-thirds say they pray every day. Eighty-five percent consider themselves Christian. Yet under the thin surface of religiosity lies a mess—at least when it comes to Christianity. Only 45 percent of those who profess to be Christian attend worship services weekly—only a percentage point different than in 1966, when God was declared dead. Almost 70 percent of evangelicals believe there is more than one way to salvation.[2] The same percentage of incoming freshman at Christian colleges say there are no moral absolutes. And 84 percent of those collegians are unable to explain basic Christian beliefs.[3]

Grabbing a Life Preserver

Clearly, something is wrong. Followers of such people as Emerson—whether they're following him intentionally or not—don't much care about Scripture or what it means to follow Jesus Christ. But even those who profess to be Christians often fail to grasp basic biblical truths or define what it means to follow Jesus Christ in purely subjective terms. In other words, they pick and choose from a smorgasbord of ideas the ones that they want to be true.

In a time of great upheaval, such intellectual and spiritual casting about is common. Capsized by the cultural wave that says there's no such thing as absolutes and that ultimate truth is relative, we're sprawling for anything to get us back on solid ground. The result is that we grab hold of whatever seems to work for the time being and, in the meantime, create a piecemeal version of true Christianity.

This book is an attempt to get you back to land. By giving at least partial answers to 10 of the most frequently posed (and most challenging, mind you) objections concerning Christianity, my hope is that you'll find yourself moving toward the dry land of a truly biblical faith. But be warned of two things. First, no book, not even this one, will give you *all* the answers. This book is just a start. And, second, the journey you are about to set out on will set you apart from the crowd. Today there is tremendous pressure to buy into the principle that all systems of belief may be true at the same time. It's reminiscent of a fascinating but disturbing experiment conducted more than 50 years ago by psychologist Solomon Asch.

In Asch's experiment, several people were shown a pair of cards with vertical lines on them. One card had a single line on it; the other had three lines of different lengths. While showing the cards, the experimenter asked each person around the table, one after another, to identify which of the three lines on the second card matched the length of the line on the first. Unknown to the participant who sat in the next-to-last seat, all the other participants were shills—they'd been instructed ahead of time to unanimously give the wrong answer. Each time the pair of cards was shown, they all picked the same wrong line.

Keep in mind that this wasn't a difficult test. The correct answer was obvious. Yet 74 percent of the time, the average subject (the lone *real* participant) went along with the group and answered incorrectly at least once. What's more, even when they didn't conform, subjects were noticeably anguished in their decision-making process. (Photos taken during the experiment document how hard it was to go against the group.)[4]

Today, Christians are much like the subjects in Asch's experiments. Academically, morally, socially and emotionally, we're at odds with most of our peers. We know which line is right, but saying so means bucking the status quo. We may be challenged by others on a daily basis in the workplace, on a university campus, during a high school biology class or even while watching our kids play at the playground. And standing up against the societal tidal waves of immorality isn't easy. In fact, claiming to believe in the absolute truths of God in today's world is more challenging than anything Asch's subjects faced. At least in his study the answer was *always* clear!

Scholar and apologist R. C. Sproul was once asked, "What is the difference between the Christian God and the gods of other religions?" In his simple yet profound answer, Sproul pointed out that the main difference is this: The God of Christianity exists.[5]

A Fight For the Truth

What this means is that the discovery of the truth, and the holding on to it, is not easy. We want it to be easy, and we sometimes wonder this: If it's true, shouldn't it be easy and obvious? But the reality is different. The Truth—with a capital T—calls us to contend. Christians believe that one of the reasons for this contest is that we are in a spiritual battle. We believe that we have a spiritual enemy who does not want us to discover and hold to the truth. Even if you are not quite to the point where you believe that, consider your own experience with things you know a great deal about. Highly competent doctors, engineers, musicians and others have knowledge and skills that, to most of us, look like magic or like natural gifts. And certainly some of us are more gifted at some things than we are at others. But most doctors, engineers, musicians and others with knowledge and skill worked diligently for years to acquire their knowledge and skills—we just weren't around to see that process. In the same way, knowledge of the battle with a spiritual enemy is knowledge acquired through a process. Live long enough as a Christian, and you'll awaken to this spiritual reality.

We know that this is true, but for some reason we expect that the much more complicated and valuable knowledge—the knowledge of the Truth of God—should come easily and simply for us. We expect to just pick it up along life's journey. But, as we have already seen, even if you don't believe in the spiritual forces fighting against that pursuit of the truth, the very culture itself is fighting against that pursuit. So your faith will not grow and thrive by merely obliging to whatever culture tells you is right. It will grow only if you make an intentional choice to stand strong and hold fast to a bigger truth.

To do so requires something deeper than head knowledge or tradition. You don't willingly stand in the face of an oncoming moral tsunami just because your parents said you should or because it's the "good" thing to do or even because that's what you've been taught your whole life. It takes believing in something wholeheartedly to risk that kind of confrontation and persecution. And ultimately, that requires knowing *why* you believe what you believe.

That's what this book is all about: discovering (or maybe just solidifying) the reason behind your faith.

One night not too long ago my wife, Angie, and I went to the opera. I'm not much of a fan of large ladies caked in makeup and wigs, singing in a foreign language, but this was different. A friend of ours, Deborah Fields, is a mezzo-soprano from New York and had the lead role in a production called *Suzannah*. We were there to support her.

"Just settle down and enjoy this," Angie said, knowing full well that I wasn't looking forward to the upcoming two hours of highbrow art. I nodded halfheartedly and slouched in my seat like a little kid. Who signed me up for this, anyway?

The truth is, I didn't fall asleep. In fact, there was even a moment that caused me to sit straight up. *Suzannah* is the gripping story of a woman falsely accused of murder. Throughout the opera, she defends her innocence and pleads for justice. And as the story reaches a climax, an exasperated Suzannah cries out to the night sky, "The truth sure has to fight hard to get believed!"

That line alone made my trip worth it. I could relate to her exasperation, having attempted to uphold the truth on a daily basis for more than 15 years. The fact is, the truth does have to fight hard these days. It's being attacked from all sides. Truth is regularly assaulted from those claiming that it is merely "religious belief." Think about it: How many times have you heard someone say, "Well that may be fine for you, but . . ."

Here's where the rubber hits the road. We are defenders of the ultimate truth. If we believe God is who He says He is, then His words are true. *They* are the truth, not some here-today, gone-tomorrow fad of thought. And that's exactly why God asks us to be defenders of His Word, the eternal truth. He's instructed us to be ready to defend our faith, to answer the questions of why we believe what we believe. In short, we're called to apologetics.

Apolo-who?

"Apologetics" is just a fancy word to describe *the reasons for what you believe*. If you've ever told an unbeliever about Jesus, you've undoubtedly used apologetics to explain your beliefs. Most likely, you've also heard a few objections to your message. Maybe one of your listeners argued that the Bible contains errors. Another person might have questioned how a loving God (if He even exists) could allow massive tragedies such as tsunamis, hurricanes or even human genocide to wipe out innocent people. All of these objections pave the way for an explanation of the Christian faith, which is essentially what apologetics is.

By definition, "apologetics" simply means "a defense." The word is used several times in the New Testament, often when Paul was defending his beliefs before a challenging crowd.[6] Like Paul, when we "do" apologetics, we are defending what we believe by showing that the content of the gospel is "backed up" by both evidence and sound reasoning.

I mentioned 1 Peter 3:15 before, the verse that encourages believers to "always be ready to give a defense to everyone who asks you a reason for the hope that is in you." The *NIV* translation uses the word "answer" in place of "defense." In the original

---

Is Apologetics Really in the Bible?

"Apologetics" isn't just a term that was made up after the Bible was written. The original Greek word from which we get the English term "apologetics" can be found in the following New Testament verses: Acts 22:1; 25:16; 1 Corinthians 9:3; 2 Corinthians 7:11; Philippians 1:7,16-17; 2 Timothy 4:16; 1 Peter 3:15.

Greek language, these words, along with "reason," imply an "analysis," a "consideration of one's position," and the "defense of a conclusion."[7] In addition to being used in the context of Paul confronting his critics, the term is repeated in Jude 3 to encourage believers to earnestly "contend" (stand up for) the faith. Whether we're simply answering someone or staunchly defending ourselves from an aggressive line of accusations, the point is that we're to be prepared to "back up" our beliefs.

An Opposing World

This isn't always easy in a world that openly rejects God. The America of today isn't the same as it was just a generation or two ago. Despite the so-called rise of "evangelical Christendom," we as a society have unmistakably moved away from our Judeo-Christian roots and into a world characterized by relativism and corruption. History says we've passed through our infatuation with romanticism and modernism, and since neither could provide solid answers to life's bigger questions, we've turned to postmodernism. So how does postmodernism answer these questions? Postmodernism simply concludes that *no* answers exist.

Don't you wish we could use that line of logic for other things in life? "I wasn't late to work, boss . . . I just decided today that my job really didn't exist—at least not until 10:30 A.M." Keep that up and you'll *really* find out whether or not your job exists.

According to postmodernists, claiming to have an absolute or right answer is both arrogant and intolerant. As a result, our Western society (which has bought in to postmodernism hook, line and sinker) is based on constantly shifting standards of right and wrong in which absolute truth is nonexistent. And as for those Christian freaks who have the nerve to say that God is absolute and that His ways are the ultimate truth—they're just narrow-minded, intolerant and naive, now aren't they?

The Rise of Apologetics

WARNING: *The following section may include
historically accurate information and could actually cause
you to become smarter. While the names and dates may bore
you a bit, trust me, there's a point to this brief history lesson
that you won't want to miss.*

It's into this culture that apologetics has grown into a near-
essential line of defense for every believer. Granted, defending
our faith has been around for hundreds of years. The apologetics movement of today can be traced to leaders who emerged in
defense of Christianity more than 100 years ago.

In the eighteenth century, the Enlightenment spread across
Europe. Today, teachings on the Enlightenment suggest that it
was a time of great flowering of the arts and technology—and
the Enlightenment was indeed a time of great innovation in
these areas. That's because one of the defining characteristics
of the Enlightenment was the rise of what eighteenth-century
philosopher David Hume called "radical skepticism." The skeptics of the Enlightenment questioned every aspect of thought
and practice in life, including philosophy and religion. So, on
the one hand, it was a time of great technological breakthrough,
as scientists, engineers and others no longer accepted the notion
that something couldn't be done. On the other hand, some of
those same people were also saying that some of the accepted
beliefs of the past couldn't be true.

Those in the intellectual realm who engaged in this skepticism and revision of ideas came to be known as free thinkers or
liberals—the word "liberal" being derived from the Latin root
liber, which means "free." Our English word "liberty," meaning
"freedom," has a similar derivation. Indeed, the liberal arts originally meant the "pursuits of a free man."

Conservatism, on the other hand, came to be the attempt to conserve the ancient beliefs. Conservatives might easily reject innovations in science and technology as well as other fields of endeavor for the sake of mere tradition. Obviously, both conservatism and liberalism in intellectual pursuits have their dangers. But liberalism and revisionism offer the greatest threats to our spiritual life, because while science and technology can and do discover new things, the most important truths about human nature are both unchanged and unchangeable throughout human history. And to pretend otherwise leads us away from, not toward, important insights about ourselves and the realities of the world.

Liberalism and revisionism were, beginning in the eighteenth century, and still are today, academically fashionable. That's why, beginning in the nineteenth century, those defending key points of Christian orthodoxy, which means "right or true teaching," certainly made their voices heard. Charles Hodges defended Genesis and the biblical account of creation in his 1878 work *What Is Darwinism?* Also, as a professor at Princeton Seminary from 1887 until his death in 1921, Benjamin Warfield was a scholarly defender of the Bible and a vocal critic of liberalism.

In 1909, a project began that would ultimately become a major development for conservative theology and apologetics in America. Two Christian businessmen funded the research and writing of a series of essays designed to defend the "essentials" of Christian doctrine, which responded directly to liberalism (often called "modernism" back then). The articles were written by conservative scholars of the day and included well-known names such as Warfield, C. I. Scofield, G. Campbell Morgan and Scotland's James Orr.

The resulting 90 articles and essays addressed many topics related to apologetics and Christian orthodoxy, including such issues as the inspiration and preservation of the Bible, the virgin birth and deity of Christ, and the reality of Jesus' miracles and resurrection. This wasn't just light Saturday morning reading! Christian leader R. A. Torrey, who studied at Yale Divinity School and later became president of Moody Bible Institute, edited the articles into a four-volume set appropriately titled *The Fundamentals*. Three million free copies of *The Fundamentals* were printed and sent to ministers and Christians throughout America—a staggering number even by today's standards.

Isn't it strange how since then the term "fundamentalist" has been assigned such a negative connotation? Today we call screaming street preachers and Islamic terrorists "fundamentalists." Obviously, the term has more than lost its original meaning, which, believe it or not, was a complimentary description of someone who affirmed the tenets of biblical orthodoxy.

During the twentieth century, liberal theology, cultural trends and conservative Christianity clashed on numerous (and often well-publicized) occasions. Most American history books highlight the battle between science and faith that escalated in the landmark 1925 Scopes Monkey Trial, in which teacher John T. Scopes was prosecuted for teaching evolution in a public school. This trial received national and international publicity largely because H. L. Mencken, the leading journalist of his day and someone who was famously and unabashedly opposed to Christianity, chose to cover the trial and to put Christian thought in the worst possible light. Other journalists followed Mencken's lead, and the so-called Scopes Monkey Trial became the dominant news story of the decade. In perhaps the first modern example of what has come to be known as "pack journalism," the reporters and editors there followed Mencken's journalistic lead, as well, and the coverage of the trial was almost uniformly antagonistic toward the Christian point of view.

Despite the positive intellectual momentum gathered by Christians during the early 1900s, the Scopes trial marked the beginning of a period in which conservative Christianity in America was perceived as being "anti-intellectual." Liberalism won back lost ground and gained momentum, while the influence and effectiveness of mainline evangelical churches waned.

Modernistic thought began to be seen as more applicable, relevant and intellectual. Christianity, on the other hand, was perceived as archaic. Despite the growth of megachurches and a Christian subculture, the turn of the twenty-first century brought with it a postmodern mentality that prevailed in both homes and churches.

"The evaporation of 4 million people who believe in this crap would leave the world an instantly better place."

—Andre Kadreskew, novelist, essayist, poet and NPR commentator[8]

The So-What Factor

What does this have to do with answering tough questions? Everything. Because in order to meet people where they are, we have to recognize and understand where they are. In other words, to address the real questions *behind the questions*, it's crucial to know why people are asking them in the first place. And a major (if not the biggest) factor stirring their queries is undoubtedly the culture that whispers the anti-God, anti-absolute untruth into their ears through every TV show, movie, radio song, news broadcast, blog posting and billboard ad. When we learn how our culture got to this point and how Christians have responded to the threats against their faith via the rise of apologetics, we can see more clearly the growing need to defend those beliefs.

So what are these daunting questions? Obviously, that's what the rest of this book is about. But before we launch into each specific question, let me quickly explain what I believe are the three overarching ones—the ones every single human deals with on a basic, often subconscious level.

1. *Does God exist?* It's a timeless classic, up there with the "Why is the sky blue?" and "Why do bad things happen to good people?" Yet it remains a question that separates the souls and spirits of humans like no other can. At some point, we all—both believers and nonbelievers—grapple with the question of how we came to exist, how life was begun. And that line of thought must always factor in a Supreme Being.

2. *What kind of God exists?* Once we establish that, yes, God does exist, the follow-up question simply addresses who this God is. Is He all-knowing? Omnipresent? Does He have a form or is He simply spirit? Is He nice, vengeful, loving or resentful? What are His thoughts and feelings regarding humanity—and more specifically, what does He think about me?

3. *How may I know this God who exists?* If we agree with the biblical depiction of who God is, it becomes clear that this God is interested in establishing a relationship with people. Since He exists, He must have been responsible for creating life. And since He created life, He must have an interest in what He has created. Not only does the Bible confirm this, it offers an open invitation to intimately know this Creator God.

Establishing a Common Ground

These questions are universal. They're inherent in our inquisitive human nature. Because of that, Christians have an opportunity to establish common, *logical* ground with any person, from the most devout believer to the most stringent of atheists. Yet it's upon these foundational questions—or more accurately, upon the *answers* to these foundational questions—that walls are erected to divide, protect and insulate. And in these strange times in which the truths of God are both welcomed and rejected more overtly than ever, religious issues are hot-button topics.

As believers, we've each been given the assignment of not only presenting the gospel but also explaining and defending it. Fortunately, God didn't leave us high and dry; we're not lacking for answers. Our beliefs are founded on the fact that God loved us and sent His Son—and this was proved further by Jesus' coming back to life after dying. The Bible confirms that the good news about Jesus isn't just based on human opinion or someone's personal preference. Second Peter 1:16 says we aren't following fables, myths or cleverly invented stories, but that there were eyewitnesses of His majesty. Romans 1:4 declares that Jesus' resurrection shows that He was the unique Son of God. (Think about it: How many other people in history have, under their own power, gone to "the other side" and come back? We'll tackle this later.) And Acts 1:3 states that after His resurrection, Christ showed that He was alive by "many infallible proofs."

I could go on and on—but that's exactly what the rest of this book contains! The important thing is that we understand the severity God places upon us knowing how to back up our beliefs with reasons. Yes, we are to have childlike faith (see Luke 10:21). But we are also to be sharp in the Word, "prepared in season and out of season" (2 Tim. 4:2, *NIV*). As we develop that precision both in spirit and intellect, we'll discover that there's no need to walk away from every argument about spiritual matters feeling defeated and inadequate. Christians can have backbones . . . and use logic too!

God Is Not Real

Common Objection:
"I don't believe God exists. How can anybody know for sure?"

Several years ago I was speaking on a college campus, presenting the basics of apologetics to a young but eager crowd. Things seemed to be going well when a professor in the audience stood up, announced himself to be an atheist and began challenging me point by point.

"Words are just sounds," he said in what seemed to be more of a public announcement than a dialogue with me. "They don't actually reflect reality. Christians use the word 'God,' but they could just as easily say the word 'shoe.' Words don't mean things. We merely attach meanings to words. The word 'God' is just a sound."

There are several subtle yet fundamental logical fallacies and practical contradictions in his positions. For example, if words don't mean things, why does he use them? Why should we believe what he is saying if words aren't an adequate vehicle by which to communicate truth? If we should be skeptical about reality, and if it's naive to think you can be sure about "ultimate truth," then why is he so certain about his agnosticism? And what basis does this skeptic have for judging the hearts, minds and motives of others? If truth is not knowable, why should we believe the position he's setting forth?

But my intention then and now is not to rail against this man, but rather to identify the point that he actually made for me: If there is no truth, as this atheist and professor asserted, doesn't that statement itself become the truth?

And that is really my point. Truth exists. This is an unavoidable conclusion. So the real question is not, "Does Truth exist?" Rather, the real question is, "What is truth, and how can we know it?"

Spreading Like a Disease

Obviously, this guy isn't alone in his thinking. Every day on American campuses, Christians are being put to the test and are flat-out opposed by professors and administrators who champion "diversity" over the quest for truth. Though diagnosing the problems at modern universities is well beyond the scope of this book, I think it is fair to say that even those who disagree with me on most other matters would agree with me that the modern public university has become a place where liberal theology and ideology are welcome, and where Christian thought is not as prevalent as it is in most of the rest of society. Liberals would argue, of course, that this is a good thing.

What is ironic here is that colleges have long been places where the pursuit of truth has been valued. When Harvard College was founded, it adopted as its motto the Latin word *veritas*, or "truth." But what is ironic is also potentially tragic, as what is at stake on campuses isn't just the fair representation of Christianity; it's the question of whether or not truth exists at all. How many times have we all heard someone like the professor above piously say, "Nothing is absolutely true."

Several years ago, a prominent North Carolina-based university was in the news over its controversial decision to prohibit a chapter of Campus Crusade to be chartered at the school. Some students apparently objected to having the respected ministry at this particular college, and opposition came even from the school's president and campus minister.

Despite this college's Christian origins (it was organized and funded by the Baptist church), despite a wide variety of other groups welcoming this chapter, and despite a significant portion of the students who favored the ministry's presence at the school, Campus Crusade was denied access because of its distinctively evangelical beliefs. A representative from the school was asked to elaborate on her campus's policy on tolerance and diversity. She responded by saying that if a certain ideology was offensive to even *one person,* that viewpoint or attitude should not be allowed on campus. (She failed to see that her cherished political correctness could not even pass its own test, for many students found *it* to be offensive.)

If you sensed a red flag rising in the back of your mind as you read through both this woman's comments and those of the professor mentioned earlier, it's because God gave you the ability to recognize a contradiction. Aristotle, often called the "father of logic," taught that there are certain things that all rational people can grasp intuitively. Indeed, God hard-wired us to instinctively recognize basic truths, things that the U.S. Founding Fathers called "self-evident." As Christians, though, we should cultivate the ability to spot the contradictions that pervade much of the conventional wisdom of our day. Since it seems no one else will, we must be the ones to point out that the Emperor is actually naked; that in the act of arguing *against* truth, skeptics are inherently assuming that something can be true (namely, their statements against truth). Whether it's on college campuses, at work or in church (God forbid), we must contend that truth not only *exists,* but that it is also *knowable* (both undeniable propositions). Beyond that, college leaders like those at the Baptist school in North Carolina need to be reminded that once you define what is or is not "acceptable" diversity, you have ceased to be diverse.

The truth-obstructing fallacies that underlie popular notions of tolerance must be exposed. Of course, explaining the gospel message and leading a person to trust Christ is another matter, but at least by helping people see the undeniable existence *of* truth, we can help point the way to a relationship with the One who *is* truth.

Life Without God

That's an especially difficult task when speaking with atheists, since they often give off an air of intellectual superiority. But as smart and innovative as they can seem at times, the truth is, atheism has been around since the beginning of human history. Humans have always tried, starting in the Garden of Eden, to push God out of the picture and establish life apart from Him. In all our arrogance, we've spent thousands of years trying to rationalize the Creator out of Creation's existence.

Every atheist carries a spiritual and emotional laundry bag full of reasons not to believe in God. Tragically, few of those reasons solely deal with God Himself. Instead, they're based on the *perception* of God, which is usually determined by extraneous factors. Many atheists, for example, have been spiritually abused. After one too many hypocritical Christians did them wrong and judged before loving, they decided that if following God looks like *that*, why be a part of it? Others have fatherhood issues because they were raised by a deadbeat or abusive dad. Whatever the issue, it's common for atheists to project those problems onto their concept of God (or lack thereof), which simply reinforces their belief that He doesn't exist.

Before we move on, let's clear something up. It's important to understand that disbelief in God can take one of two forms: atheism or agnosticism. Atheism says there is no God, while agnosticism believes you can't know for sure if there's a God or not. An atheist completely rules God out; an agnostic, perhaps intent on being more "open-minded," only rules out the possibility of certain knowledge of God.

Both are wrong. But I must say that I have more respect for an honest agnostic than I do for an avowed atheist, because to be a true atheist requires not only a rejection of God, but also an active acceptance of many beliefs that, I would argue, are much more intellectually difficult to believe in than God!

We'll talk more about that later. For now, let's examine some of the fatal flaws found in both atheism and agnosticism.

"There are no infidels [atheists] anywhere but on earth. There are none in heaven, and there are none in hell. Atheism is a strange thing. Even the devils never fell into that vice, for 'the devils also believe, and tremble' (James 2:19). And there are some of the devil's children that have gone beyond their father in sin. But when God's foot crushes them, they will not be able to doubt His existence. When He tears them in pieces and there is none to deliver, then their empty logic and their bravados will be of no avail."

—Charles H. Spurgeon[1]

Mr. Know-It-All . . . I Think Not!

It is important to realize something about being an atheist that even most atheists fail to acknowledge and that is that atheism requires omniscience (complete knowledge of everything).

If you don't believe that, then consider this: An atheist is making a positive assertion that there is no God. The only way that anyone could make such an assertion would be to presume that he knew everything about everything. Otherwise, there would always be that possibility that God in fact existed, but that He was just outside of knowledge or our ability to know.

The last time I checked, *The Guinness Book of World Records* still hadn't discovered a human with the world record for knowing it all. Obviously, it's not possible. Yet atheists say that nothing exists outside of the material world, placing them in a God-like position. I'm sure Columbus, Magellan, Descartes and any other explorer would chuckle at the arrogance of this notion. Even people during their time who thought the world was flat still believed there was something else out there.

In reality, this intellectual position is the height of arrogance. But atheists tend to disguise this arrogance with intellectualism. In his best-selling book *Cosmos,* renowned evolutionist/atheist Carl Sagan proclaimed, "The Cosmos is all that is or ever will be." Sagan believed humans should move beyond the age-old belief that life had been the special creation of a personal God. He spoke for multitudes of evolutionists in asserting that humans were simply an evolutionary accident, "a mote of dust in the morning sky." Such admissions, Sagan wrote, were "not, I think, irreverent, although they may trouble whatever gods may be."[2] (Sagan didn't mean the God of the Bible. Rather he meant what he believed to be man-made gods and superstitions.)

In following Sagan's line of thought, that the "Cosmos is all that is or ever will be," consider what would be required for someone to accept with certainty that this is true. Again, to rule out even the possibility that a God exists above and as a creator of the Cosmos would require omniscience on the part of the person making that claim. Often, the language of atheists communicates a kind of false humility, as we could see in the quote by Sagan, when he described humankind as a "mote of dust in the morning sky." But this artful and falsely humble language masks the reality of this thought process. Atheism is an attempt to make humans into gods. That, in a way, is the ultimate irony: Atheists, in their denial of God, cannot help but replace the truly omniscient God with a cheap imitation—themselves!

Still, atheists will argue that faith in the God of Scripture is simply naive—a more primitive system of thought, if you will. Their logical blind spots remind me of a line from the Will Smith movie *I, Robot*. The actor plays a cynical cop in the future who seems to be the only person on Earth open to the slight possibility that a robot could develop beyond the scope of its creator's design. Teamed up with a theory-driven, numbers-based scientist, Smith becomes exasperated by the woman's refusal to accept anything outside her system of belief. After hitting an impasse one too many times, he yells at her, "You are the dumbest smart person I know!" With their adamant denial of a Supreme Being, truly many atheists are the dumbest smart people I know.

Can't You See the Contradiction?!

Agnostics aren't that different, as their beliefs are built on contradictory assertions. As we've just discussed, an atheist can't truthfully say that God doesn't exist since he doesn't have all knowledge. An agnostic, on the other hand, claims that you can't know for sure whether God exists or not. But think about it: By claiming that you can't really know anything for sure about God, you've done the very thing! In making such a statement, you therefore know *something*—namely that He can't be known. In other words, it's a contradiction to say, "One thing I know about God: You can't know anything about Him." Yet that's exactly what an agnostic says. Talk about being double-minded!

I've spoken on many college campuses throughout the years. And without a doubt, when presenting this side of the argument against agnosticism, I've had a couple of fervent students fire back, "Okay, I'll buy into the notion that God exists. But that's all we can know about Him. It's impossible to know anything specific beyond that."

My usual response goes something like this: "Wait a minute! Listen to what you're saying, because in your own words you've already established a couple of things here: one—He exists; and two—you know something about Him. In saying that you can't know anything about God, you're claiming to know at least *one thing* about Him."

"One walking with me observed, with some emphasis, 'I do not believe as you do, I am an agnostic.' 'Oh,' I said to him, 'that is a Greek word, is it not? The Latin word is ignoramus.' He did not like it at all. Yet I only translated his language from Greek to Latin."

—Charles H. Spurgeon[3]

Not Up For Debate

Don't you find it interesting that the Bible never addresses the question of whether God exists? From the first words of Genesis through the last letters of Revelation, the existence of God is a given. "Well, sure—*that's* a given," some would argue. "It's the Bible. Of course it wouldn't argue against this since it's the foundational document for those who believe God indeed exists." That's true. But those same believers also understand that God's big enough to handle any question. He's fully capable of dealing with the most extreme doubters who claim He's nothing more than a human-concocted fairy tale.

So what does Scripture have to say about those doubters, the atheists and agnostics who claim that God doesn't exist and can't be known? "The fool has said in his heart, 'There is no God'" (Ps. 14:1). Could it be any clearer? The Bible doesn't even address the atheists' flawed ideas, except to call them foolish!

God's existence is both undeniable and necessary—and not just for Christians. In the following sections, we'll deal with some of the "proofs" that demonstrate this truth. No, they're not passionate, emotional appeals to believe in this unseen God; they're simply logic-based reasons that appeal to our common sense, because, strangely enough, God created us with common sense. Though often we may be fooled by lies and delusions, as I stated earlier, humans are hard-wired with the ability to recognize contradictions. We're prone to spot things that just don't make sense.

Remember the story of *Alice in Wonderland*? One of the reasons people love the tale is because of its nonsensical nature. It's full of contradictions that border on the absurd—yet that's the very reason we enjoy this fanciful whirlwind of an adventure. We chuckle when the Mad Hatter makes such statements as, "Have some tea, there isn't any," because we know this makes absolutely no sense. Throughout the book, author Lewis Carroll (who was an ordained minister and whose real name was Charles Lutwidge) is simply playing with the English language—and with our sense of reasoning—to make a point. He turns things upside down and backward to show the foolishness of illogical reasoning. Likewise, no matter how passionate or "intellectual" we get in our arguments, some things just don't add up.

It's no different with what our culture calls the fundamental question of spirituality: Does God exist? As you'll see through the following proofs, that's as silly as asking if water is a liquid, or if the sky is blue, or if gravity is real.

1. Every Effect Has a Cause

We all learned in science class that every effect has a cause. An effect without a cause is an impossibility. Stated another way, you can't have an outcome or consequence without having something to cause that result. Likewise, it's hard to imagine the universe not having a source behind it. Even atheists believe that the universe is a massive cause. Evolutionists believe that that cause came from a big bang millions of years ago. Christians credit the source as the Almighty God. Either way, both science and Scripture acknowledge that the universe had a beginning. Science has proven it through such means as the Hubble telescope or the Red Shift. Scripture simply states it as understood truth.

So the question up for debate isn't whether the universe has an origin, it's who—or what—prompted that beginning. Imagine you're sitting in your living room, enjoying a peaceful afternoon while reading the paper. Suddenly, a baseball flies into the room, shattering your window. Obviously, your first question wouldn't be, "How did that get here?" It would be, in a highly bothered tone, "Who did this?!" The baseball didn't just smash through your window for no reason. Some agent acted upon it, causing a "disturbance in the force" that ruined your perfectly good afternoon.

The point is, the universe couldn't have just "arrived" without a force behind it. And unlike the remote possibility that a pitching machine spat a baseball into your living room instead of an actual person, it's virtually impossible that a universe was just spat out by an inanimate force. It took a Person, a Someone. Holding the Bible at its word, we Christians believe that Someone to be God, the Great Cause.

2. Every Creation Has a Creator

In the same way, it's impossible for something to be created void of a creator. Something that's made has to have a maker. Both creationists and evolutionists agree that life didn't just suddenly appear; it was made by something (a Big Bang) or someone (God). The universe is a creation, and the earth's life cycle clearly proves that.

Going one step further, however, Genesis proves that God is responsible for creation. The first two chapters serve as "the history of the heavens and the earth when they were created, in the day that the Lord God made the earth and the heavens" (2:4). Obviously, some people think of the biblical creation account as a fairy tale that lacks truthful substance. Yet if all creation serves as proof of a Creator, who—or what—else could be responsible?

3. Every Design Has a Designer

Watch a sunset. Stare at the waves of the ocean. Examine a leaf or a flower. Hold a newborn baby. Our eyes don't have to travel far to find proof that the earth was intricately designed. The world around us is bursting with wonderful, breathtaking design. And following suit with the previous two "proofs," this implies that behind the design is an ultimate designer.

But there's more. The complexity of the earth's designs—from the mesmerizing patterns of nature to the awesome uniqueness of a DNA strand—tells us that this designer is *intelligent*. The patterns of life are obviously not mindless happenstance.

Before the mountains were brought forth, or ever You had formed the earth and the world, even from everlasting to everlasting, You are God (Ps. 90:2).

Think of it another way: Cars go through a systemized process in their formation. They don't just build themselves from iron and elements found in soil; they're formed and fashioned in automobile factories. Likewise, concertos are birthed through composers, paintings come from painters and inventions come from inventors. Each product is uniquely created by the hands of a person. If we acknowledge that this world consists of incredible and intricate designs, how can we not point to the hands of a designer?

4. Communication Requires a Communicator

Scientists agree that the universe is constantly communicating with us. When we hear this, most of us imagine some half-crazed researcher spending decades listening to static noise from outer space, waiting for some abnormal yet distinct pattern or variance. For example, the 1997 movie *Contact*, based on Sagan's 1985 book, gave us a glamorized version of the legitimate search for extraterrestrial intelligence. In it, Ellie (played by Jodie Foster) is monitoring radio waves and signals from outer space, listening for some sort of ordered, encrypted sequence in the midst of static. She and other scientists eventually decipher a signal that is, as they describe it, "not local." As a result, they surmise that a complex, ordered pattern "can only come from an intelligent source."[4]

Such communication can be found in our everyday existence. Consider the fact that the blueprint for who we are is intricately coded within the DNA molecules of each of our bodies. In other words, the DNA contained in every cell within your body contains information. It's filled with "instructions"—complex, coded information. Obviously, information can't be communicated unless there's a communicator—and in this case, an *intelligent* communicator—delivering the information.

5. Every Law Has a Lawgiver

If you've ever studied sociology, you know that there are some things that people everywhere recognize—they're universal. One of those is smiling, and another is the existence of moral law. No matter where you go in this world, people inherently recognize the difference between right and wrong. We are born with a conscience that gives us such a filter. Obviously, we don't always *do* what's right—but we *know* what's right.

"Everyone knows certain principles. There is no land where murder is virtue and gratitude vice."

—J. Budziszewski, educator and author[5]

Imagine traveling to 10 separate islands out in the ocean. On the first island you visit, you discover an unspoken list of dos and don'ts. Even without an official government to rule over them and establish laws, you've noticed that the locals have established their own code of ethics that prohibits such things as murder, theft, adultery, molestation . . . it goes on. As long as everyone abides by these "rules," everyone's happy.

When you move on to island number two, you're amazed to find virtually the same moral code, despite the fact that none of these people have ever had any interaction with those on the previous island you visited. Again, certain boundaries have been naturally established.

Coincidentally, the third island you visit has virtually the same "laws" as islands one and two, even though these people again have been completely independent and secluded from the other two. This pattern continues for all 10 islands you visit. And though it's amazing to think of the similarities, it raises several valid thoughts: If the people on all 10 of these islands have never had any interaction with each other, yet all 10 have a similar moral code, wouldn't it be within reason to assume there's a natural inclination aiding the establishment of these laws? Since those on all 10 islands have virtually the same idea of what is right and wrong, isn't it logical to presume that this idea came from a third party?

Don't believe it? Think the scenario is a little too theoretical and idealistic? Believe me, it's not that far-fetched. In C. S. Lewis's *The Abolition of Man*, the author documents cultures throughout all history, presenting some of the common threads that bind every civilization. Among these commonalities are the notions that you shouldn't murder, steal, sleep with your neighbor's spouse, and so forth. On the flip side, all cultures esteemed telling the truth, being kind, acting selflessly, and so forth. In every case—from the Phoenicians to the Egyptians to the Greeks to the Romans to twenty-first-century civilization—humans shared a vehement reaction against injustice: theft, looting, rape, murder, pillaging and the like. Meanwhile, they all innately affirmed heroism, altruism and self-denial.

Lewis's study (and others by Christian apologists and sociologists) proves that different people groups and cultures, though having no contact with each other, nevertheless had similar moral codes and ethical structures by which they lived. That's not to say that humans always *do* what is morally right; Lewis and others assert that all cultures intuitively *know* what is right.[6]

"A great many of those who 'debunk' traditional or (as they would say) 'sentimental' values have in the background values of their own, which they believe to be immune from the debunking process."

—C. S. Lewis[7]

Since human knowledge of moral law appears to be ubiquitous, and since different cultures all seem to know moral truth—whether civilized or primitive, urban or rural—the source of moral knowledge must be absolute, rather than subjective. In other words, morality isn't just a social mores (a "cultural accident" as evolutionists would assert) but it is intrinsic and from some outside source (i.e., God). There must be an outside lawgiver!

If, then, we've established that we all know the law but don't always live it out to perfection, then that equates to breaking the law. And if we're honest, we must admit that in breaking the laws, we've offended the lawgiver. The moral code, then, doesn't just point us to the lawgiver, it also reveals our need for forgiveness and a Savior! (We'll get to that later.)

It's Time to Get Personal

After briefly delving into these five "proofs" (and obviously, there are more—those are just the most frequently addressed issues), let me say something that may rock your boat a little: Don't get hung up on any of these as your proof that God exists, because essentially, these can only get us so far in knowing the "who" behind the "what." These evidences simply lead us to a fuzzy, nebulous Supreme Being who is responsible for all of life. In fact, we could have the god of Star Wars—the god of some mysterious "force"—based on what we've discussed so far.

Fortunately, there's more. We're not left hanging by an unknown God. Quite the opposite, in fact. If there's one thing we can be sure of, as revealed through creation, history, Jesus Christ and the Bible, it's that God is personal.

"But I'm still not sure I believe in Jesus or the Bible," you say. That's fine. We'll get there. For now, let's review some things we've already established in order to arrive at a new and fundamental point.

We concluded that both science and Scripture agree that the universe has a beginning. Was this beginning caused or uncaused? We know that an uncaused effect is impossible; it doesn't exist—clocks don't wind themselves, baseballs don't throw themselves. So the universe was intentionally caused. If that's the case, we can assume this "Causer" must be personal, since He created personal beings.

There Must Be Something More

Say the name Friederich Nietzsche and you immediately think of a single phrase: "God is dead."[8] The outspoken atheist, who once called himself the Antichrist and labeled his brand of thought "philosophizing with a hammer," coined the famous declaration as part of his adamant denial of God's existence. For much of his life, Nietzsche argued that there was no God, no afterlife and that existence amounted to nothing more than life in this world. But prior to his death, Nietzsche longed for permanence beyond this life. Arguing for what he called "eternal return," he attempted to retain a belief in naturalism yet hoped for a world continually being reformed and reborn.

Nearing his death, Nietzsche said, "The eternal hourglass of existence is turned over and over, and you with it, a grain of sand."[9] In his final years, it seemed that this tenacious and influential atheist could not come to grips with his own belief that his existence—and personhood—would one day be snuffed out. His example shows that atheists long for what scholars call *transcendence*—something beyond this natural, mortal world.

How so? Well, simply put, if God isn't personal, then He's less developed than we are. God must *at least* be personal because He created humans to be personal. You and I have a will; we have emotion, personality, volition and ambition. If God isn't a personal God, then He's not as sophisticated as us, and we (the effect) have eclipsed Him (the Cause). That's not rational. And that also means it's safe to say that because God is in fact the Causer/Creator/Intelligent Designer/Communicator/Lawgiver who, in each case, is above the effect/creation/design/communication/law, then He is indeed personal.[10]

Okay, Now That We're on a Friendly Basis . . .

So what does all this have to do with the price of eggs in China? Remember, the atheist says God doesn't exist. We've already proven the flawed rationale behind that one. Meanwhile, the agnostic says that God may indeed exist, but that He can't be known. We've talked about how that's a contradiction; but now that we know that God is a personal being, there's more to add. And here's where it gets good.

Not only does God reveal Himself as personal, but He also invites us to know all about the rest of Him. God is a *revelatory* God. How do we know He's really out there, that He really wants to know us and isn't just tricking us into being mindless robots that say and do whatever He wants? Simply put, because He's already proven Himself. He's shown us. He has—and still is—revealing Himself to the world.

How is He doing this? There are four significant ways He shows Himself. In a general way, He proves Himself through:

- *Creation*—The universe itself isn't just proof of His existence; it's a snapshot photo of who He is.

- *Conscience*—The basic moral code that's innate in all of us shows us God's standards, which reveals His character.

God has also proven Himself through more specific means:

- *Scripture*—Virtually every page of the Bible paints an up-close and personal portrait of God.

- *Savior*—Jesus Christ came as God in flesh to show us firsthand who God is, unlike anything or anyone else could.

Don't worry if you're not sold on these yet, specifically the Bible and Jesus parts. We'll address those later in the book. For now, my point is simply to show you that God doesn't have to be viewed as some out-there, far-off Supreme Being who can't be described. He is personal, which means there's more of Him that we can know, more about Him that we can discover. Not only can He be searched, He *wants* to be searched (and found)—specifically by you!

Summary Response

Reasons for the existence of God:

A philosophical reason
A moral reason
A scientific reason
A biblical reason
A Christological reason
A personal reason

Creation Is a Myth

Common Objection:

"What about evolution? Couldn't God have created us but used evolution to do it?"

He wanted to be a minister, but after setting sail in December 1831 for what became a five-year voyage along the South American coastline and across the Pacific Ocean, Charles Darwin veered far off course. The 22-year-old son of a country doctor kept his Bible nearby throughout his travels to remind him of his past. Yet by journey's end, he would return a different man. Darwin did not deny that there was and is a God. He often referred to God in his writings. But he became convinced that if God had anything to do with the world around him, His impact was indirect. God may have set things in motion, Darwin believed, but from there He had pretty much left things alone.

Fast-forward 150 years and Darwin's notions have stirred the waters of controversy within this nation like no other issue. Many have called his revolutionary book *The Origin of Species* one of the most influential books ever published. Indeed, its message has shifted the gaze of an entire nation and has profoundly affected the world. In essence, Darwin's work helped establish a naturalist framework for life that minimized and ultimately banished the possibility of God's influence. Things change with time, it states, regardless of God being in the picture. And with the release of *The Descent of Man*, evolutionism firmly established itself as traditional creationism's forceful opponent by declaring that man had descended from apes.

Though Darwin was aware that sharing his views was the equivalent to "confessing a murder" at the time, I doubt he or any of his contemporaries could have predicted the far-reaching ramifications of his assertions. Nor could they have foreseen how rapidly those theories would become a cultural "truth." In the Introduction, we mentioned the infamous Scopes Monkey Trial of 1925—*Tennessee v. Scopes*—which upheld the law that made it illegal to teach evolution in public schools. Yet by 1987 the tables had completely turned when the Supreme Court ruled that teaching *creationism* in the same setting was unconstitutional. And in December 2005 a federal court went so far as to declare unlawful the mere *suggestion of the possibility* of a higher being's influence ("intelligent design") while teaching.

How'd We Get Here?

Based on the rulings of a handful of judges, you'd think our nation had thrown her arms around Darwin and kissed God goodbye . . . all in the name of science. To most people, it now appears that believing in God stands in direct opposition to scientific progress. To deny creationism—or even the idea of intelligent design (which we'll get to later)—is "true science," while affirming creationism is simply old-fashioned, outdated and irrelevant religion.[1] So has science made it impossible to still believe in the creation? Are we a product of a mighty God or a muddy glob? Are we made in God's image or mud in God's absence?

That's what this chapter is all about. Obviously, entire books have been written debating evolutionism versus creationism. We'll certainly discuss both sides, weighing several evolutionary arguments. But, for the purposes of answering this chapter's most common objection to Christianity, I'd like to also discuss the deeper issues of faith in the unknown and why we're so apt to dismiss what we can't see or prove with scientific data. I also want to tackle the question of whether a Christian can believe in God and evolution at the same time. Before we get started, however, we need to clarify the term "evolution."

Soup Anyone?

As I already mentioned, Darwin's initial idea of evolution described a process: Over many generations of life, through random mutations and natural selection, species adapt to their environment. The fittest survive while the less fit go extinct. The longer a species can pass along its best characteristics from generation to generation, the better its chances of hanging around on Earth. Darwin's famous observations of rare species on the Galapagos Islands provided the basis for his theory.

Yet Darwin and his followers took his theory one step further to explain life's origins. And in a single colossal leap, he went from naturalist observer to speculative theorist. His theory of evolution made a sweeping claim that the relatively small adaptations he observed within some species could—given enough time—actually result in the creation of new species. But even more than that, the theory of evolution now teaches that life—the biological processes of procreation and biological regeneration that we see in living creatures—could have randomly evolved from nonliving material.

Not only does evolution attempt to explain apes and humans as having a common ancestor, it also attempts to explain the beginnings of all of life. And it's in this extensive context that I'll use the term "evolution."

Simply put, evolutionism is the belief that life arose by the combination of chance, time and a primordial "soup" (the mucky pond of glob from which the first living cell supposed-ly emerged). Evolutionists believe that all of life as we know it came about by mute forces often called "blind chance" and "natural selection." Life changed into other forms of life, which developed and mutated. Fortunately, the best aspects of those changes were somehow introduced into the gene pool that, over millions of years, contributed to both you and me. And it all traces back to our original home, the primordial soup.

Evolution's parent worldview is naturalism, which holds the notion that everything can be explained via pure science. Virtually all evolutionists are naturalists, meaning they believe that no questions about this world may ever be answered with a supernatural explanation. To them, the concept of God is about as logical as a flying cow. And as a result, God is to be ever left out of the equation.

"Can the mind of man, which has, as I fully believe, been developed from a mind as low as that possessed by the lowest animals, be trusted when it draws such grand conclusions?"
—*Charles Darwin*[2]

Them's Fightin' Words

When it comes to talking about the questions surrounding the origin of life, many evolutionists work hard to make sure that the rules of the discussion are set in advance. Having dialogued with hundreds of evolutionists over the years, I would say that many prefer "rationed inquiry" over "rational inquiry." Regardless of any evidence that you may present, most evolutionists will not allow God to be a part of any answer or view. And when your evidence points to God, be warned: Their reactions can become heated.

When someone doesn't accept your conclusion yet can't refute your data, he may resort to sarcasm, slander or verbal attacks in an attempt to discredit your view. This is sometimes called an *ad hominem* attack, which means "to the man." Basically, it's a tactic of belittling the messenger when you're unable to disprove his message.

What I find fascinating, however, is that this isn't just occurring over water-cooler discussions; it's taking place on a national scale. In the spring of 2005, a much-publicized conflict erupted in Topeka, Kansas, regarding whether or not students in public school science classes should be allowed to hear a view opposing evolution. Topeka students were told that evolution is a theory believed by some scientists—and that equally credible scientists theorize that the universe is the product of an Intelligent Designer. The reaction from hard-core evolutionists was anything but tepid.

"It is ridiculous to backtrack to the 1700s and subvert our education to superstition and religion," voiced one natural history museum director. Steven B. Case, head of the Kansas science standards committee, got a little more personal: "Intelligent design has no scientific credibility, but they very effectively market a controversy. They speak well in sound bites. 'Intelligent design' is a good one. They never specify a designer."

A *Washington Post* article even stated that "scientists warn that introducing challenges to evolution in the public school curriculum will weaken education and, as one paleontologist put it, open Kansas to ridicule as 'the hayseed state.'"[3]

In the state's higher education institutions, the story was much the same. In reaction to a Kansas Board of Education ruling that called Darwinian evolution a "flawed theory," the University of Kansas began offering a class to "explain" how anything other than evolution was merely myth. "Creationism is mythology," said religious studies department chair Paul Mirecki. "Intelligent design is mythology. It's not science. They try to make it sound like science. It clearly is not."[4]

"All truth passes through three stages. First it is ridiculed. Second it is violently opposed. Third it is accepted as being self-evident."

—Arthur Schopenhauer, evolutionist and atheistic philosopher

Unscientific Scientists

We're told to trust science (and by implication, scientists) as the ultimate means of attaining truth. If we can prove it with tangible data, it must be true. What is often forgotten, however, is the degree to which some scientists' work is influenced (if not predetermined) by their naturalistic views. Recent stories are revealing more that science isn't always as objective, pristine or unbiased as evolutionists would have us believe:

- A *Washington Post* story reported that a "surprising number" of scientists and researchers "engage in troubling degrees of fact-bending or deceit, according to the first large-scale survey of scientific misbehavior."[5]

- A recent confidential questionnaire among scientists revealed that more than 15 percent admitted to having changed a published result to suit the desires of a financial backer. More than 5 percent admitted tossing out data that contradicted previous research or some intended result. And 13.5 percent said they'd used research methods or approaches they knew would not give accurate results.[6]

- In Korea, a panel of scientists determined that researcher Hwang Woosuk presented misleading information regarding his work with stem cells. The group, most of whom worked with Hwang, said his research involving stem cell lines "cannot be some error from a simple mistake, but cannot be but seen as a deliberate fabrication." In light of the revelations, the panel said that it would also investigate Hwang's other research.[7]

Turning the Tables of Logic

Obviously, it's unfair to argue against evolution based solely on the corruption of a few scientists. So let's look at the problem from as close to a purely logical point of view as we can.

First of all, it is important to understand that even if evolution could occur in the way that today's evolutionists say it did, the set of circumstances that must have existed are extraordinarily specific. Nothing would exist as we know it if certain life-sustaining variables were altered in the most minute way. Astro-physicist Lawrence Krause, for instance, wrote that if the force of gravity were changed by 0.00000000000000000000000 000000000000001 percent, both planet Earth and the sun would be nonexistent.[8] Research proves that "if gravity were only slightly stronger . . . stars would flame so fiercely they would burn out in a single year; the universe would be a kingdom of cinders, devoid of life. If gravity were only slightly weaker, stars couldn't form and the cosmos would be a thin, undifferentiated blur."[9] Indeed, it appears that the universe is uniquely structured and specifically designed for life as we know it.

This fact alone does not prove the existence of a creator, or Intelligent Designer, but it begins to help us see how improbable it is that life as we know it could have evolved from nonliving material, and that nonliving material could have been generated in just the right proportions and with the precise amount of energy to convert to living material. Again, even by accepting the assumptions of evolution—that mutations and "natural selection" could eventually create life from nonliving material, and that lower forms of life could evolve into higher forms of life—you still have to let enough time go by, and enough "incidents" must happen in order for the evolution to occur.

Today, many reputable scientists now believe that the amount of time that must have gone by, and the number and characteristics of these mutations are so specific, that it is unlikely that they occurred by accident.

"It seems like a tremendous coincidence that the universe is suitable for life."

—*Charles Seife, science journalist and author*[10]

Fred Hoyle was an astronomer who, in 1953, figured out the preconditions necessary for the formation of carbon. He reasoned that the likelihood of this happening by chance, as the Big Bang theory suggests, were phenomenally low, and this revelation led him to convert from atheism to a belief that the universe reflects a "purposeful intelligence." Hoyle admitted that "the probability of life originating at random is so utterly minuscule as to make the random concept absurd."[11] Again, Hoyle's conclusion does not prove that there is a God or an Intelligent Designer; however, it is important to note that Hoyle's intellectual honesty about evolution led him to the conclusion that it, too, required a great act of faith. Hoyle's conclusions, then, suggest that it takes as much or more faith to believe in evolution than it does to believe in a purposeful Designer.

And Hoyle is not alone. Over the past 150 years, paleontologists have examined an estimated 1 billion fossils representing 250,000 species. Millions of these fossils have been found within the earth's Cambrian strata of rock, a layer said to be the oldest in which fossils of living creatures have been found. (Evolutionists believe that the Cambrian rock is between 600 and 500 million years old.) Interestingly, all of these remains found within the Cambrian rocks are fossils of fully formed creatures. Life—complete, fully mature creatures—appears *en masse*.

This "Cambrian explosion"—a term referring to the puzzling fact that these creatures seemed to have "burst onto the scene"—brings to the surface a fact particularly damning for evolutionists: Each of these living forms appears suddenly—completely developed—in fossil record, not through gradual transition as evolution would suggest. Even Charles Darwin recognized that the earth's rock does not reveal his long-sought "intermediate varieties." Regarding this complete lack of transitional fossils, he admitted, "This, perhaps, is the most obvious and gravest objection which can be urged against my theory."[12] Hard-core evolutionist Richard Dawkins added, "It is as though they were just planted there, without any evolutionary history. Needless to say, this appearance of sudden planting has delighted creationists."[13]

"None of those depicted images, in all those museum displays and textbook drawings, can be backed up by even one example in the fossil world. How much anti-evidence does it take to overcome evolutionist rhetoric and bluster?"

— *Duane Schmidt, Darwinist expert and creationist author*[14]

Gene, Would You Mind *Doing* Something?

Then there's the question of gene mutation. The theory of evolution depends, in part, on new features arising through beneficial gene mutations. It's assumed that biological activity and changes within genetic material occurred, with ultimately positive outcomes. For evolutionists, much depends on the possibility of beneficial, upward change within the chromosomal material of living things.

But for positive changes to be introduced into living forms—and certainly for entirely new species to emerge—*additional* genetic information is necessary. The same genetic information repeated (even repeated millions of times) would simply yield the same physiological result. Mere change doesn't mean an *increase* in genetic information.

This fact has been yet another thorn in the side of evolution, especially when considering the colossal amount of time in which they admit this change would need to take place. Doctor and author Geoffrey Simmons explains:

> Once in every 10 million cell divisions, a cell makes a copying mistake. The chance of the mistake passing into the next generation is one in two. The odds are six to one that it will disappear by the tenth generation, and 50 to one that it will be gone by the hundredth generation. According to [anthropologist] F. B. Livingston, it would take approximately 20,000 generations, or 400,000 years, for an advantageous gene to spread among the hominid populations of the Pleistocene Era. If we are descendants of the famous Lucy, the australopithecine skull found in Ethiopia in 1974, and thought to be 3 million years old, then there would have been time for only seven advantageous genes to have changed.

That's barely enough of a change to tell a difference, let alone make a monkey into a person.[15]

Evolutionists may hopefully appeal to "beneficial mutations" for support, but the fact is, new genetic information or new life by mutation has *never* been observed.

Testing the Monkeys

British biologist Thomas Huxley was a staunch defender of evolution—so much so that he was often referred to as "Darwin's Bulldog." In responding to those of his day who questioned the likelihood of "blind chance" being able to result in order and life, Huxley infamously said that if you let monkeys type on a keyboard for a long enough period of time, eventually one of them would come up with the works of Shakespeare.

In 2003, researchers at the Plymouth University in England decided to put Huxley's assertion to the test. In cooperation with the Paignton Zoo, university faculty and students placed a computer keyboard inside a facility containing six Sulawesi macaques (monkeys). And what did they find? Lead researcher Mike Phillips recorded that one male beat on the keyboard with a rock. "Another thing they were interested in was in defecating and urinating all over the keyboard," he wrote. The monkey experiment didn't yield Huxley's predicted works of Shakespeare, nor anything readable. "Obviously, English isn't their first language," Phillips observed.[16]

In the same way, the primordial, pre-biotic "soup," plus ages of time, would not yield the complex, ordered universe that we see around us. The faith that evolutionists place in natural selection or chance is not supported by empirical evidence. The unstable legs of improbability on which evolution was built actually serve as a mere indicator to the presence of a designer. And as "scientific fact" resurfaces as nothing more than prefabricated fiction, the origin of the universe becomes not so much about "what" but about "Who."

"In Darwin's day, the origin of life was a very easy problem. Life was basically a little blob of Jell-O enclosed by a membrane. It would have been very easy for it to come about by spontaneous generation. Darwin knew nothing about molecular biology. Nowadays, the simplest cell is more complicated than any human artifact . . . It's a marvel of miniaturization and engineering that is going on in the cell. Darwin had no conception of this. Why should we think that his theory can account for this new body of facts?"

—Dr. William Dembski, professor, author and intelligent design expert[17]

Can I Get a Witness?

If you're starting to doubt evolution, you're not alone. Several prominent writers, scientists and thinkers have started to admit the problems with the sweeping assumptions behind the theory. Regarding the earliest origins of humanity, *Time* magazine's senior science writer, Michael Lemonick, concluded, "The only certainty in this data-poor, imagination-rich, endlessly fascinating field, is that there are plenty of surprises left to come."[18]

Professor Leslie E. Orgel, one of the world's leading evolutionary biochemists, commented on the likelihood of life forming from a chemically rich blob: "It is extremely improbable that proteins and nucleic acids, both of which are structurally complex, arose spontaneously in the same place at the same time. Yet, it also seems impossible to have one without the other. And so, at first glance, one might have to conclude that life could never, in fact, have originated by chemical means."[19]

Meanwhile, despite being an evolutionist, Jeffrey Schwartz, professor of anthropology at the University of Pittsburgh, admits, "The formation of a new species by any mechanism has never been observed."[20] And scientist N. A. Takahata seems to put the nail in the coffin when he concludes, "We have no direct access to the processes of evolution, so objective reconstruction of the vanished past can be achieved only by creative imagination."[21]

Every Design Needs a Designer

Before launching into a more in-depth analysis of intelligent design (ID), let's review some of the facts that point to the necessity of a creator being. First, we know that the universe had a beginning. That's an accepted truth whether you're a Bible-thumping Christian or a Darwin-spouting evolutionist. Second, there's no fossil data that conclusively supports evolution. Archeologists have discovered and analyzed the bones of specific creatures, none of which are morphing species that evolved from crude versions of their selves.

Third, there are numerous examples of the universe's "fine tuning," all of which point to its inherant nature as a creation rather than a creator. In other words, change the smallest of details and we'd end up with a completely different world. The sheer impossibility that this universal precision was by chance proves both the absurdity of evolution's stance and the realistic probability of the ID theory.

Finally, humans can simply look at a cell to thwart any notion that we were formed from a mere glob. Each cell is irreducibly complex; entire parts are unable to evolve without the presence of other parts. Such complex cohesion is highly unlikely in a "by chance" environment. Add to this the problem of "chirality." Former evolutionist Ralph Muncaster explains that "chirality is the term for the observed phenomenon that all amino acids in DNA are of the same molecular orientation. This is vital to the making of DNA—and its origin by chance is mathematically impossible to explain."[22]

Biologists are keenly aware of the complexity of life, and most know of the astronomical odds against even one protein molecule having arisen accidentally. Yet for evolutionists, the elements of our origin remain as follows:

primordial soup

+

random, natural interactions

+

lots of time

=

life, intelligence, order and consciousness

The leap from an unobserved, unrepeatable past to dogmatic belief in evolution is one that most seem willing to make. Many scientists (for various reasons, including professional and philosophical ones) maintain belief in evolution despite known problems with the theory. (It's interesting to note, however, that since the 1960s, there is a noticeable reluctance among evolutionary scientists to include chance as an impetus behind the origin of DNA or proteins—this, despite the fact that evolution remains as strong as ever in the public's eye.[23]

What ID Is and Isn't

Now that we've established those strikes against evolution, it's important to point out what ID *does not* attempt to do.

ID doesn't seek to turn biology classes into theology lessons, nor is it a presentation of "how to know Jesus as Savior." It's not, as some opponents claim, about "sneaking religion into the classrooms." ID simply acknowledges that complex designs (like those found prolifically throughout biological life) do not come about randomly but arise only from intelligent sources.

So what's the point of arguing for an Intelligent Designer? Simply this: It brings logic back into the discussion of origins. Belief that something can come from nothing, belief that chaos birthed order, and belief that lifeless matter produced consciousness is not only counterintuitive, but it's also irrational. And yet that's exactly the state in which evolutionary dogmatists have kept American classrooms for decades.

ID isn't only logical; it's also a plea for rationality. It asserts that when you find complex, ordered design, it is reasonable to believe that such purposeful, complex and effective arrangements come about through the intervention of an outside agent. Stated another way, we can say ID is about two basic (and rational) tenets: (1) Intelligent causes exist; and (2) Intelligent causes can be detected using empirical science.

For centuries, scientific methods have been used to detect "works done by an outside agent" or "intelligent sources." Scientific disciplines that examine empirical data and posit the presence of outside force include criminology, archaeology and forensic medicine, just to mention a few. A forensic pathologist, for instance, examines a body, is able to determine the cause of death, and can determine that an outside causal agent inflicted the fatal blow. Other scientific fields involve the same inclusion of an "outside force." The recent Cornell University SETI (Search for Extra-Terrestrial Intelligence) Project involves looking for basic patterns in outer space—in this case, they're looking for radio signals and waveforms exhibiting rudimentary order.

Nowhere else in the physical world do we see information arising accidentally. We know from every other context of life that things like order, complexity, patterns, encryption, intentionality, interdependency, specificity, information and purpose—in other words, design—and that these always come about through the agency of a *mind*. Phrased another way, *design* comes from a *designer*. If it's unscientific to conceive an intelligent source as being the cause behind the astounding intricacies of biological life, then certainly forensics or the SETI project can't be classified as science, either.

Evolutionists, however, plead for special exemptions when it comes to explaining biological life: "*These* designs (DNA, amino acids, proteins, irreducibly complex organisms) didn't require a designer!" Evolution explains the past as design by accident and sees the present as exhibiting no design. What I call "semantical gymnastics" are all a part of a naturalist's effort to keep any talk of God removed from the discussion over origins.

"An honest man, armed with all the knowledge available to us now, could only state that in some sense, the origin of life appears at the moment to almost be a miracle, so many are the conditions which would have to have been satisfied to get it going."

—Francis Crick, Nobel prize-winning biologist who contributed to the discovery of DNA[24]

Those Crazy Creationists!

Creative semantics sometimes gives way to downright rudeness. Evolutionist Richard Dawkins says this of those who doubt evolution: "It is absolutely safe to say that, if you meet somebody who claims not to believe in evolution, that person is ignorant, stupid or insane (or evil, but I'd rather not consider that)."[25] Other jibes against those who disbelieve evolution are a bit subtler. In his piece "Darwin in Mind," Tanner Edis, a writer for the *Skeptical Enquirer* (a vocal anti-ID, anti-creationist publication), tries to discredit ID by attempting to make it appear ludicrous. Edis compares creationists inferring the existence of God to that of "proving the existence of the abominable snowman."[26] In the quest to defend naturalism at any cost, some evolutionists invoke false comparisons (that they surely must realize are invalid) in an attempt to make belief in the supernatural appear ludicrous.

As a result, it's easy to point out the faulty logic behind evolution arguments. For instance, a comparison that places the likelihood of God's existence and activity on the same plane as that of an abominable snowman would contain a number of flaws:

- Sound reasoning—consistently followed—infers that an ultimate, uncaused, eternal, omnipotent being must exist. Logic in no way makes the same inference about an abominable snowman.

- There is no reason to assume that an abominable snowman (if it exists) would possess attributes commensurate with those of deity.

- Nothing that's known about the physical world infers that reality is the product of an abominable snowman. That is, reality doesn't seem to have been the product of a finite, bear-like creature from Earth's polar regions.

- The vast, well-ordered, consistently operating universe; complex life forms; human consciousness—all of these (and more) do argue for the existence of God. Reality

in no way appears to argue for an abominable snowman as its cause, while knowledge of the world around
us does argue the existence and intervention of an outside, objective, intelligent force (i.e., God).

Clearly, the adamant mind-set of evolutionists is maintained as a result of *faith*, not evidence. Stated in plain English,
evolution is a faith system. Whether God is included in your
picture or not, you have to accept your view of the universe's
origins on faith or trust. We can't travel back in time to observe
what happened as the universe began. The Big Bang is an unrepeatable phenomenon; none of us was there to witness it. So
whatever we conclude about the beginning of the universe we
have to conclude on faith.

---

*"Is it possible that suddenly, without intending to, we have stum-
bled upon the scientific proof of the existence of a Supreme
Being? Was it God who stepped in and so providentially crafted
the cosmos for our benefit?"*
—George Greenstein, astronomer[27]

Do Faith and Science Collide?

That brings us to a burning question among some Christians:
Is it possible to be a Christian and an evolutionist at the same
time? Obviously, a professing believer accepts the biblical creation account as truth; otherwise they'd be concluding that
God's Word contains false accounts (we'll cover more on this
in later chapters). And yet I find it fascinating how many
Christians incorporate evolution into their belief of how the
universe began. *Maybe buried between the early verses of Genesis are*

the unrecorded periods of evolutionary progress. Maybe dinosaurs existed before Adam and Eve ever came along, making God's creation "days" actually thousands or millions of years. Or maybe God created the world, then left it up to the "survival of the fittest."

The truth is, we're not sure of the time frame surrounding the creation account. The Bible leaves much unspecified, while also adding that "with the Lord one day is as a thousand years, and a thousand years as one day" (2 Pet. 3:8). What we can be assured of, however, is the *who* of this mysterious equation: "In the beginning God created the heavens and the earth. The earth was without form, and void; and darkness was on the face of the deep. And the Spirit of God was hovering over the face of the waters" (Gen. 1:1-2). There was no blob formed from nothingness. No sudden carbon-based bang of a universe sprouting from emptiness. No, all of life's *alpha* was God Himself, who is eternal. It was His Word that spoke the heavens into existence, His Word that formed the earth and its inhabitants. And it is His Word that allows evolutionists and creationists alike to breathe their next breath.

Because that, when they knew God, they glorified Him not as God, neither were thankful; but became vain in their imaginations, and their foolish heart was darkened (Rom. 1:21, KJV).

Could God have used evolution to create the world? Not by the Bible's account. Obviously, species have progressed, adapted and morphed into various stages of advancement, while others have died out. But that viewpoint of evolution is but a sliver of the entire package. It's the PG-rated preview to an R-rated movie. And it's sold millions of believers and unbelievers alike with its "practical" element, luring them into the theater of evolution only to be doused with the filth of a dark, godless view of life.

Of course things change to survive, just as Darwin asserted. Yet evolution involves more than just change—let's not forget the Big Bang, amoebas, blobs, monkeys and ape-men. To incorporate the entirety of Darwin's shoddy philosophy into God's masterpiece of life is to insult the Maker.

Why Not Just Take the Bible at Its Word?

In the beginning God created the heavens and the earth.
GENESIS 1:1

In six days, the Lord made the heavens and the earth,
the sea, and all that is in them.
EXODUS 20:11

Thus the heavens and the earth, and all the host of them,
were finished. And on the seventh day God ended His work
which He had done, and He rested on the seventh day.
GENESIS 2:1-2

I'll never forget the time I emceed a conference our ministry was hosting in Connecticut. I was sharing the stage with an elite group of apologists including Josh McDowell, Lee Strobel, Norman Geisler, Ravi Zacharias, Erwin Lutzer, John Ankerberg, Gary Habermas, and others—truly a rare event to have all these great Christian minds together in one place. Yet it was fitting, since we were in the heart of Ivy League territory. The audience of more than 2,100 people consisted of students and professors from nearby Yale and Brown universities, as well as self-described Marxists, searchers, skeptics, atheists, liberal protestants and even a Hindu priest. Add to this, the event was being broadcast via satellite across America, with more than 120 remote sites watching "live." Without anyone saying it, we knew the question of the day was whether Christianity could hold up in such an intellectually charged environment.

At the end of the conference, we opened up the floor for an impromptu Q&A session. More than 150 people lined up to pick the brains of these scholars—or, as expected, to get into an intellectual sparring match with them. But it was one question and answer that I remember most vividly that day. A young man approached the mic and asked, "Can a person believe in evolution and still be a Christian?"

Dr. Geisler fielded the question: "Sure, a Christian *could* believe in evolution, but why? Evolution isn't supportable scientifically or biblically."

The man pressed the question: "Can't I be a Christian *and* an evolutionist?"

The apologist's response was priceless: "I suppose you *could* . . . I know people who are Christians but believe lots of cockamamie things!"

The truth is, evolution and Christianity just don't mix. The Bible (which we'll establish as truth in the next two chapters) plainly shows why evolution couldn't have even been a "tool" God used for creation. Aside from the creation account in Genesis, we have several verses speaking of creation coming directly from the hand of God:

- Jesus quotes from the Genesis passage in Mark 10:6, saying, "From the beginning of the creation, God 'made them male and female.'"

- In Colossians 1:16-17, Paul writes, "For by Him all things were created that are in heaven and that are on

earth, visible and invisible, whether thrones or domin-
ions or principalities or powers. All things were created
through Him and for Him. And He is before all things,
and in Him all things consist."

• John 1:10 explains, "He [Jesus] was in the world, and
the world was made by Him, and the world knew Him
not" (*KJV*).

• We also know that there was no death in the world until
sin was introduced (see Rom. 5:12,14; 1 Cor. 15:21),
which means humans—the original sinners—had to
have already been created.

These are just a sampling of the truths laid out in the Bible
regarding evolution. If you're still trying to reconcile the two,
however, I'd ask a deeper question: Why? Is there a reason why
you can't accept—whether by faith or by scientific reasoning—
the creation account as is? Consider Jesus' probing words: "For
if you believed Moses, you would believe Me; for he wrote about
Me. But if you do not believe his writings, how will you believe
My words?" (John 5:46-47).

---

*But even if our gospel is veiled, it is veiled to those who are per-
ishing, whose minds the god of this age has blinded, who do
not believe, lest the light of the gospel of the glory of Christ,
who is the image of God, should shine on them (2 Cor. 4:3-4).*

Blinded Me with Science

In this chapter, we have addressed two basic models of origin:
evolution and creation. Either has developed by continuous

natural processes or through divine invention and care. Each model is a complete worldview, a philosophy of life and meaning, a view of both origin and destiny. Neither creation nor evolution can be verified or falsified by the scientific method alone, since neither can be tested or observed in a lab experiment. And because of that, either model must be accepted by faith.

Nevertheless, each model is a scientific model, since each seeks to explain within its framework all the real known data of science and history. Creationism is at least as nonreligious as evolutionism, yet evolutionism is as "religious" as creationism.

Some say that creation isn't testable, can't be repeated in a laboratory and is therefore unscientific. Guess what? That's completely irrelevant, since evolution also can't be repeated in a laboratory or tested under laboratory conditions and, in fact, has *never* been observed in all of recorded history. And think about it: How can creation—the event—be observable if it was completed in the past?

Yet another assertion is that creation is based on supernatural processes, whereas evolution is based on natural processes and is therefore more scientific. Answer me this: When (and by whom) was it ever determined that "science" should be defined as strictly "naturalistic"?

As you can tell, the arguments go on and on and can get pretty exhausting. But essentially, it boils down to this: Can chance produce intelligence? Could accident result in purpose? Can nonlife create life? Can something come from nothing? Is chaos the mother of order?

And if you've reached this far in the chapter and answered yes to any of those questions . . . I'll pray for you!

Summary Response

Reasons against evolution being a
correct view of origins:

It is a flawed theory.
The presence of bias.
The lack of evidence.
A scientific impossibility.
Professional disagreements.
Moral repugnance.
Social detriment.

The Bible Is Not Completely Authentic

Common Question:
"How do I know the Bible is really true?"

Can you imagine a world without measurement or weight? A world without systems standards of any kind? Think what would happen if there were no alphabet, no metric system, no currencies, no hours or minutes. Imagine if 1 plus 1 didn't equal 2 but instead 3, 12.863 or 39—and only on a sunny day.

Without these things, there would be anarchy. Commerce, science, music, medicine, engineering and almost all other disciplines would be much more difficult—if not impossible—to pursue. But more than that, a world without standards is really not a world without standards; it is—rather—a world in which there are many standards, defined by whomever, however he or she sees fit. For example, if I wanted to own your house, I could offer you my No. 2 leaded pencil because, hey, in my mind that pencil sure is worth a lot. And if the words "muggleforth sienkleton ropersplatten" don't make sense to you—well, that's your fault, because they add up in my book.

Obviously, we need certain standards to function in life, whether those standards are time measurement, established rules for language, or simply the acceptance that a dollar is worth 100 cents. Without acknowledging and accepting these principles as truth, the world would be pretty chaotic.

It is interesting that we accept this notion—that standards are necessary—in most every area of our culture, but that when it comes to the moral state of our culture, we are often quick to reject that standards are necessary or important. Even the most avowed secularist and relativist is likely to agree that certain mathematical laws are reliable across time and cultures, such as the Pythagorean Theorem. But often these same people will contradict themselves and say that there are no absolutes. They will say that morality cannot be considered absolute and unchanging. As we talked about in earlier chapters, our culture has gone from having a decidedly defined understanding of right and wrong to adhering to a "whatever goes" worldview. Moral relativism rules the day.

The Trinity of Dissenters

How did we get to this condition? Though this moral transition involved a succession of events, concepts and people, I believe three individuals stand out. The first is Friedrich Schleiermacher, who is often referred to as the "father of liberalism." Schleiermacher was a pantheist, meaning he believed that everything was god, that everything was spirit. He loathed orthodox, historic Christianity, in which God became a man to redeem us from sin. In other words, you could say this guy had a theological axe to grind. In 1799, Schleiermacher wrote *On Religion*, which kicked off theological liberalism and established the viewpoint that denied the Bible as God's Word. In essence, his efforts undermined the view of God as communicator.

In 1859, a second individual, Charles Darwin, added insult to injury with his monumental *The Origin of Species*. As Darwin ushered in the age of evolution (which we discussed last chapter), he also undermined the view of God as creator and moral authority. Finally, in the 1960s came Joseph Fletcher, who established the concept of moral relativism with his *Situation Ethics: The New Morality*. For 2,000 years, moral rights and wrongs had been absolutely defined because they had descended from the character of God. Malachi 3:6 for example finds God Himself declaring, "I the Lord do not change" (*NIV*). Also, the writer of Hebrews states that "Jesus Christ is the same yesterday and today and forever" (13:8, *NIV*).

With God no longer part of the equation by the 1960s, morality went up for grabs. And yet morality is inextricably tied to the core of who God is. What's wrong today is wrong tomorrow, and what's right yesterday is still right today. Rights and wrongs don't change for one simple reason: God doesn't change. He is truth. He is right. So by pulling God out of the concept of morality, moral relativism undermined the view of God as its author.

Now, there are some who say, "Wait a minute, there's lots of stuff in Leviticus that God said was wrong, but today you Christians say is okay." And that's a valid response—as far as it goes. But it's important to note that scholars of all theological varieties agree that the laws of the Old Testament fall into three categories: the ceremonial laws, the hygienic laws and the moral laws. The ceremonial laws were laws specific to the Jewish Temple and to the worship of God in that temple. These laws, clearly, do not apply to Christians today. The so-called "hygienic laws" were given to protect God's people from things that were bad for them. For example, prohibitions against pork were made in the Old Testament to protect God's people from diseases that at that time were common and deadly. But, again, these laws were not for all time.

The moral laws of God are those given to us because to violate them would be to violate God's standards and order for the universe He created. These laws are unchanging because they reflect the character and mind of God, whose character and mind are unchanging.

It is interesting and a bit odd that many people today use this argument—that because some laws in the Old Testament are not valid today, then none of the laws are valid and the Bible is not a source of morality and truth—to reject the overarching truth of Scripture. It is odd because we would never tolerate that objection in other matters. For example, all states set a minimum driving age—usually age 16. In other words, we say to a 14-year-old, "It is wrong for you to drive." But we say to a 16-year-old, "It is not wrong for you to drive."

You might say that our restrictions on the 14-year-old are the equivalent of a hygienic law. It is given for his or her well-being. There is an overarching principle that we might think of as a moral law in this situation as well, and that law could be stated this way: "Love your children and guard their safety. Don't give them more responsibility than they are capable of exercising safely."

Obviously this example is imprecise, but it does help us to see that it is possible to accept an unchanging absolute moral law while at the same time accept the idea that some laws are given for a time and a place. The important thing is that we remember that we ourselves are not the lawgivers. God Himself is the lawgiver.

If God is not the communicator, if He's no longer the creator, and if He's renounced as the arbitrator between right and wrong, then the result is chaos. And that's precisely what we see today. Yale University law professor Steven Carter aptly stated, "We are paying the price for having banished religion from public life."[1] And at the core of this unruly state is a scene reminiscent to the Garden of Eden. Just as Adam and Eve believed the lie that God's words were no longer completely true, we've bought into the belief that God's Word—the Bible—is a fairy-tale-like fabrication. Through the loud objections of Schleier-macher, Darwin, Fletcher and others, our culture has turned its ear, sided with these unmerited claims, and ultimately tossed the Bible out the window. But by denying the inspiration and authority of Scripture over our lives, this conclusion has been reached without a solid, factual basis. I can't say this strongly enough: The Bible is true. It is correct. It is God's Word.

"The mere fact that the Bible claims to be the Word of God does not prove that it is such, for there are other books that make similar claims. The difference is that the Scriptures contain indisputable evidence as being the Word of God."

—Josh McDowell, evangelist and apologist[2]

Club Doubters

Tragically, it isn't just staunch atheists, evolutionists and panthe-ists who are crying foul on the Bible being God's Word. Many Christians have their doubts about the Bible's inerrancy. *Surely there must be some mistakes after thousands of years of copying and trans-lating. Surely there has to be a book or two that wasn't intended to be part of the Bible—and wouldn't that in turn put the whole thing in question?*

The assumption is that because it's an old book, the Bible must have errors in it. (Funny thing is, few people can even point to a specific "error" in question. We'll tackle that issue in the next chapter.) But we cannot forget this crucial point: The *age of the Bible* and the *content of the Bible* are two completely differ-ent issues. Antiquity does not automatically imply error. In this chapter, we'll stick exclusively to discussing the first of those two issues: authenticity.

Few Numbers, Big Gaps

Many ancient manuscripts have been discovered that contain all or part of the Bible. These include scrolls, parchments of skin, and papyri. In the ancient world, papyrus was used just as we use paper today. Love letters, tax receipts and copies of Scripture are some of the more than 100,000 copies of ancient papyri that have been discovered. By examining the style of handwriting, an expert papyrologist can date a writing sample accurately to within 25 to 50 years of when the text was written.

Because of the large number of discoveries and the accuracy with which ancient manuscripts can be analyzed, we can get a clear picture of how the Bible compares to other accepted ancient documents. The fact is that the Bible has better manuscript credentials than those of any other ancient literature or written work.

Consider this: Ancient copies and portions of the Bible that have been found far outnumber those of any other ancient work. How far? Seven manuscripts of the writings of Plato are known to exist today. Greek historians Thucydides and Herodotus each have eight copies of their works around today. Roman historian Livy has 10—the same number of manuscripts known to exist of Caesar's *Gallic Wars*. And the writings of historian Tacitus clock in with 20 existing copies. The record for the greatest number of ancient scripts known to exist goes to Homer, with his *Iliad* having been preserved in 643 known pieces.[3]

Yet what's so peculiar in light of the relentless attacks against the Bible is that not one of these manuscripts' validity has been questioned. Though existing only in a relatively small number of copies (with the exception of Homer's novel), each of these ancient writings has been accepted by historians and classified as unquestionably authentic. Add to this that there is a time gap to be considered for every copy of an ancient manuscript (biblical or secular). Each contains a lapse between the actual events recorded and the date when the earliest known manuscripts regarding that event were discovered. For instance, almost 1,450 years lay between the time of Aristotle's life and the earliest-dated surviving manuscripts that include his teachings. Another 1,300-year gap exists between the time ancient writer Herodotus lived and our discovery of the existing copies of his work. For Pliny the Younger, the gap is nearly 800 years, and for Homer, it's a "mere" 500 years.

Evidence by the Numbers (and Years)

So how does the Bible stack up to these universally accepted ancient manuscripts? Let's examine the basic facts. The last book of the Old Testament, Malachi, was completed almost 400 years before the birth of Christ. The Jews translated the entire Old Testament from Hebrew to Greek around 200 B.C. Before the discovery of the Dead Sea Scrolls (which we'll talk about later), the oldest known copies of the Old Testament in Hebrew were from about A.D. 900.

This text, known as the Massoretic Text, was meticulously preserved by the Jewish scribes (called Massoretes) who copied the Hebrew text with incredible care. It is complete, unchanged and available for us in its original form to this present day—a fact that's confirmed by comparing translations of Latin and Greek manuscripts to ancient Hebrew copies. But because of the more than 1,300-year time lapse between the writing of the Old Testament and the discovery of this Massoretic Text, many skeptics in the 1700s to early 1900s proposed that the writings had surely been altered. Their doubts stirred up the myth that remains today, which says the Bible was tampered with and "corrupted," and that it therefore is unreliable as the written Word of God.

At the peak of this cynicism came what many have called the greatest archaeological find of all time. In 1947, in a valley west of the Dead Sea, a shepherd boy stumbled upon a group of caves housing several unimpressive clay jars. What was inside these vessels, however, was most impressive. The ancient documents, now commonly known as the Dead Sea Scrolls, dated from about 150 B.C. to A.D. 70 and contained the writings of scholarly Jews known as the Essenes. The Essenes lived in a community called Qumran (not to be confused with the Islamic book the Koran).

Most likely hidden by the Jews from hostile Romans, the Dead Sea Scrolls survived many centuries and yielded ancient copies of every Old Testament book, with the exception of Esther. They were also much older than any other of the oldest known copies of the Old Testament books. Of special interest was the fact that the Dead Sea Scrolls contained a complete transcription of Isaiah, a book originally written about 750 B.C. and was hotly debated by scholars. (Controversy over Isaiah's authorship and content was probably due to the fact that Jesus Christ seems to clearly fulfill the book's predictions about Israel's promised Messiah.) The Dead Sea copy of Isaiah (from about 150 B.C.) was in complete textual agreement with what previously had been the oldest known copy of the book (from about A.D. 900). Despite the 1,000-year difference, examination of the Isaiah copies affirmed that the Old Testament content had indeed been faithfully preserved. In fact, as the Dead Sea Scrolls were scrutinized side by side with the previously oldest manuscript found, scientists were amazed to find that not a single word—not a single punctuation mark—had been changed. Obviously, the Dead Sea Scrolls validated the trust Christians place in the accuracy of the Old Testament.

I tell you the truth, until heaven and earth disappear, not the smallest letter, not the least stroke of a pen, will by any means disappear from the Law until everything is accomplished (Matt. 5:18, NIV).

New Testament, Same Evidence

With numerous data to validate its authenticity, the Old Testament is far more trustworthy than the most unquestioned of ancient texts. Its strength is in its quality of preservation. But what about the New Testament? How credible is it when stacked up against these accepted works? Once again, the facts speak for themselves.

New Testament documents don't come to us in 7, 8, 10 or even 643 copies, but *thousands.* This second part of the Bible has been preserved and corroborated via more than 24,000 discovered manuscripts! More than 5,000 of these are Greek manuscripts, providing ample attestation for content of the biblical books.

What about the time gap between Jesus' life and our copies of the Gospels? How much time passed from the writing of the New Testament books to our earliest surviving copies of the same? Yet again, the evidence is almost astounding when compared to other ancient works. The time gap is not measured in centuries, as it is with these other texts, but mere years. "Every book of the New Testament was written by a baptized Jew between the 40s and the 80s of the first century A.D. (very probably sometime between about A.D. 50 and 75)," confirmed the late William F. Albright, a renowned expert on biblical archaeology.[4]

Philosophy and religion professor Winfried Corduan asserts, "No other ancient document equals the New Testament when it comes to the preservation of manuscripts, both in terms

of number and closeness in time to the original autographs."[5]
In his classic book *Our Bible and the Ancient Manuscripts*, biblical
archeologist Sir Frederick George Kenyon added that:

> The number of manuscripts of the New Testament, of
> early translations from it, and of quotations from it in
> the oldest writers of the church, is so large that it is prac-
> tically certain the true reading of every doubtful passage
> is preserved in some one or other of these ancient
> authorities . . . This can be said of no other ancient book
> in the world.[6]

---

*"The evidence for our New Testament writings is ever so much
greater than the evidence for many writings of classical authors,
the authenticity of which no one dreams of questioning . . .
If the New Testament had been a collection of secular writings, their authenticity would generally be regarded as beyond
all doubt."*

—F. F. Bruce, English scholar [7]

While the Old Testament's strength is its quality, the New
Testament stands unmatched by its sheer quantity. As with the
entire Bible, questioning the credibility of the New Testament
text would require tossing out the validity of *every other* ancient
manuscript ever found. That's the extent to which God's Word
stands up as the most reliable, verifiable source ever written.

Gospel Truth

Before we move on to examining more proof of the Bible's
authenticity (as if it's warranted), I want to briefly discuss the
Gospel accounts of the life of Jesus. Perhaps no four books have

Individuals Referencing New Testament Texts as God-Given Scripture

Psuedo-Barnabas (A.D. 70-130): cites Hebrews and 1 and 2 Peter

Clement of Rome (died c. A.D. 98): cites James, Hebrews and 2 Peter

Ignatius (A.D. 110): cites Philemon

Polycarp (A.D. 110-150): cites 1 Peter and 1 and 2 John

Hermas (A.D. 115-140): cites Hebrews, James, 1 Peter, 1 and 2 John and Revelation

Papius (A.D. 130): cites Revelation

Iraneus (A.D. 130-202): cites Hebrews, 1 Peter, 1 and 2 John and Jude

Collections of Scripture and Canons Affirming New Testament Books

Muratorion Canon (A.D. 170): contains all of the New Testament except Hebrews, James and 1 and 2 Peter

Barococcio Canon (A.D. 206): contains all of the New Testament books except Revelation

Apostolic Canon (A.D. 300): contains all of the New Testament books except Revelation

Athanasius's *39th Festal Letter* (A.D. 367): contains all of the books of the New Testament

Councils Affirming the New Testament Books

Council of Nicea (A.D. 327): recognized all New Testament books but questioned James, 2 Peter, 2 and 3 John and Jude

Council of Hippo (A.D. 397): affirmed all 27 New Testament books

Council of Carthage (A.D. 397): affirmed all 27 New Testament books

Second Council of Carthage (A.D. 419): again affirmed all 27 New Testament books undergone as much scrutiny as Matthew, Mark, Luke and John—obviously in an effort to disprove Christ. A number of non-Christian belief systems (such as Islam and Scientology) assert that the facts about Jesus have been distorted and the Bible changed from what was originally intended. It's often supposed that the New Testament documents were written decades, even centuries, after Christ lived, with numerous revisions being introduced along the way. This line of thought has even made its way into pop culture via conspiracy-themed books (and movies) such as Dan Brown's *The Da Vinci Code*, Michael Baigent's *Holy Blood, Holy Grail* and other popular writings by members of the Jesus Seminar. These works perpetuate the belief that power-hungry men fought over the Bible's content, with the "winners" of the struggle earning the rights to do final edits.

The fact of the matter is this: More than 24,000 copies of New Testament manuscripts have been found. The Rylands Papyri, which contains the book of John, was written a mere 25 years after the life of Christ. The Chester Beatty Papyri, which contains the entire New Testament, was penned only 50 to 100 years after the original events. I could go on and on listing the numerous findings, each of which were written only years after Jesus walked on the earth. Credible scholars from a variety of theological backgrounds point out that the basics of the Christian message were known, understood and circulated within three to eight years after Christ's crucifixion.[8]

Add to this the miraculous fact that all of these discovered texts have matched one another word for word, as was the case with the Old Testament. Yet somehow, despite the astounding evidence of both time gap and quantity, the Gospels remain questioned by doubters, while other far less validated ancient texts go unquestioned. Today belief that the New Testament accounts about Jesus were cobbled together long after the fact has reached urban legend status. But when held under historical scrutiny, it's obvious that such an argument is itself a tall tale.

"The amazing thing about all these 'debunk Jesus' books is that they accept as much of the recorded Gospels as they find convenient—words like 'God is love'—then ignore or repudiate other parts of the same document which contradict their notions."

—Louis Cassels, United Press International religion writer[9]

Found in the Ground

The Bible's validity doesn't just come from how it compares to other ancient texts, as outstanding as that attribute is. There is also substantial archeological proof that attests to the authenticity of God's Word. Recently, archeologists unveiled an inscription at the renowned Jerusalem site known as Absolom's Tomb, where for centuries it was believed King David's son was buried. A barely visible inscription on the monument, however, identifies the landmark as the burial place of Zacharias, John the Baptist's father.[10]

Close by is another inscription now referred to as the Simeon epitaph. Luke 2:25-35 tells us of a Simeon who saw the young Jesus in the temple and recognized Him to be the promised Messiah. This inscription, found on one of the three prominent funeral monuments built in the Kidron Valley, is a verbatim reading of verse 25. "This is believed to be the first discovery of a New Testament verse carved onto an ancient Holy Land shrine," says inscription expert Emile Puech, who translated the writings. It is believed that these inscriptions were carved in the fourth century by Byzantine Christians who traveled the Holy Land marking biblical sites. Bishop Eusebius (A.D. 260-340, called the "father of church history") and Jewish historian Josephus both affirm that biblical figures Simeon and James were buried in the Kidron Valley. Prior to the discovery of this monument, no documentation had been found regarding Simeon's death.[11]

While these two findings in and of themselves don't prove the Bible's authenticity, they're part of the myriad of archeological discoveries that verify people, places and events mentioned in the Word.

Some of the Old Testament events and places verified by archeological discoveries include the following:

- The city of Jericho.

- The city of Nineveh.

- Ur, which had Ziggurats (similar to what scholars believe the Tower of Babel would have resembled).

- Babylon—a clay fragment was uncovered here with the following description of one ziggurat: "Offended the gods, was destroyed at night . . . people scattered with speech made strange."

- Meggido—long thought to be merely legend, Solomon's horse stables have been located. They were called "horse cities" and could hold 450 horses each (see 1 Kings 9; 2 Chron. 8).

- The tomb of Joseph (see Gen. 50).

- King Jehoiachin sites—a king of Judah who reigned only three months (see 2 Kings 25). In the area of Hebron, three separate inscriptions have been found referencing this short-lived king.

- Sanballat and Tobiah (from the time of Nehemiah)—
the Zeno papyri and the Elaphantine papyri, both
dated to within 40 years of the time of Nehemiah, reference "Sanballat, Governor of Samaria" and "Tobiah,
Governor of Amman."

- City of Tyre (see Ezek. 26:3-14, written about 597 B.C.)—
Ezekiel prophesied that the city of Tyre would be
destroyed. At the time of his prophecy, Tyre was one of
the greatest seaport cities of the ancient world. The
prediction was partially fulfilled in 586 B.C. through a
siege led by Nebuchadnezzer. But Ezekiel's prophecy
had said, "more than one nation will come against it."
Around A.D. 330 the prophecy was completed when
troops led by Alexander the Great finished the destruction of Tyre. Today, the old location of Tyre is actually
underwater in the Mediterranean Sea. Though there is a
city today named Tyre, it is a different city in a different
location, built hundreds of years after the destruction of
the biblical city of Tyre. In other words, as predicted, the
biblical city of Tyre was never rebuilt and to this day
remains a place "to spread fishing nets."[12]

Some of the New Testament places verified by archeological discoveries include the following:

- Bethany
- Bethlehem
- Bethesda
- Cesarea
- Cana—in A.D. 725 an inscription was found referencing
"Kenna (Cana), near Nazareth" and mentioning "the
miracle of the wine."

- Capernaum
- Emmaus
- Gennesaret
- Jericho
- Jerusalem
- Nain
- Nazareth
- Sychar

Reasons to Trust the Bible

If you're still not convinced of the Bible's authenticity, allow me to offer seven more undisputable facts that may change your mind. (And if it's the so-called "errors" of the Bible that are causing your doubts, we'll address these and more in the next chapter.)

1. Fulfilled Prophecies

Hundreds of Bible prophecies have been fulfilled, specifically and meticulously, often long after the prophetic writer had passed away. For example, the prophet Daniel predicted around 538 B.C. (see Dan. 9:24-27) that Christ would come as Israel's promised Savior and prince 483 years after the Persian emperor would give the Jews authority to rebuild Jerusalem. At the time of the prophecy, Jerusalem lay in ruins. Yet this was clearly and definitely fulfilled hundreds of years later.

The Bible is full of extensive prophecies dealing with individual nations and cities and with the course of history in general—all of which have been literally fulfilled. More than 300 prophecies were fulfilled by Christ's first coming. Other prophecies deal with a wide variety of subjects, including the spread of Christianity and of various false religions.

Mathematics and astronomy professor Peter Stoner was a skeptic of the Bible, and to test its prophetic accuracy (which is often considered a litmus test of any major religion), he observed 48 major Old Testament prophecies concerning the Messiah that would come. Out of these 48, he considered just 8 of these (dealing with the Messiah being born in Bethlehem, His persecution, the attempts on His life and so forth) that established severe parameters to govern who this Messiah would be. Using the principles of probability, he concluded the following: The chance that any man might have lived and fulfilled all 8 prophecies is 1 in 10^{17}; yet the chance that any one man fulfilled all 48 prophecies is an astounding 1 in 10^{157}.

Of course, this sort of exercise neither proves nor disproves that Jesus was the Messiah, nor that the Bible is true. But such an exercise does highlight that the Bible is in a separate category from other religious and mystical books. The prophesies of the Bible—unlike the prophesies of other religions—are both *specific* and *verifiable*.

So what does this mean? Stoner believed it meant that either these prophecies were given by inspiration of God or that the prophets wrote them just as they thought they should be, even though they knew they'd have a 1 in 10^{17} shot at having *any* of them come true in *any* human hundreds of years later. Yet, as Stoner observed, *every single* prophecy came true in Jesus Christ. This revelation ended up changing Stoner's life and convincing him of the reality of both God and the Bible.[13]

There is no other book, ancient or modern, with these sorts of specific and verifiable prophesies—which ultimately come to pass and are true! The vague and usually erroneous prophecies of people such as Jeanne Dixon, Nostradamus and Edgar Cayce can't compare; neither can other religious books such as the Koran or the Confucian Analects. Only the Bible manifests this remarkable prophetic evidence, and it does so on such a tremendous scale as to render completely absurd any explanation other than divine revelation.

2. Historical Accuracy

As we've already seen, the historical accuracy of the Scriptures is in a class by itself, far superior to the written records of Egypt, Assyria and other early nations. Archeological confirmations of the biblical record have been almost innumerable in the last century. Archeologist Dr. Nelson Glueck, probably the greatest modern authority on Israeli archeology, commented, "No archeological discovery has ever controverted a biblical reference. Scores of archeological findings have been made which confirm in clear outline or in exact detail historical statements in the Bible."[14]

3. Scientific Accuracy

Another striking feature of the Bible is that many of the principles of modern science were recorded as facts of nature in the Bible long before scientists confirmed them experimentally. A sampling of these includes:

- Roundness of the earth (see Isa. 40:22)
- Almost infinite extent of the sidereal universe (see Isa. 55:9)
- Law of conservation of mass and energy (see 2 Pet. 3:7)
- Hydrologic cycle (see Eccles. 1:7)
- Vast number of stars (see Jer. 33:22)
- Law of increasing entropy (see Ps. 102:25-27)
- Paramount importance of blood in life processes (see Lev. 17:11)
- Atmospheric circulation (see Eccles. 1:6)
- Gravitational field (see Job 26:7)

None of these are stated in the technical jargon of modern science, of course, but in terms of the basic world of man's everyday experience. And, again, it is important to remember that the

Bible is not a science text. The Bible, understood at its most basic level, is the story of God's creative and redemptive work on behalf of mankind. The Bible does not explain to us all that there is to know about the world God created. Rather, the Bible is a book that is intended for our salvation.

Nevertheless, both mankind and God's creation exist in time and space, and when the Bible mentions and describes the natural world, we discover that what the Bible says is completely in accord with our most modern scientific understanding. It's significant to note, also, that no real mistake has ever been demonstrated in the Bible—and that includes science and calculations. See the next chapter for more on this.

4. Indestructibility

Our modern Western society cringes at the notion of censorship. And yet the Bible has been the subject of countless censorship attempts. Throughout history, various leaders have attempted to eradicate Scripture from the public mind-set. In A.D. 303, Roman emperor Diocletian ordered all Bibles destroyed. Only 20 years later, Constantine offered a reward for any remaining Bibles. (Within 24 hours more than 50 complete copies were brought to him.) In 1199, Pope Innocent III ordered all Bibles burned, and anyone who tried to hide or stow away a copy of Scripture faced house arrest.

When Joseph Stalin came to power in the 1920s, he ordered that all the Bibles be purged from the U.S.S.R. —this, ironically, despite the fact that one of the most valuable Old Testament manuscripts known at that time was housed in the state-run library in Leningrad. Even one of the twentieth century's most brutal dictators, and the leader of an openly, officially atheistic state, could not bring himself to fully eradicate the Bible.

Regardless of the era, the Word of God hasn't just persevered but it has often flourished while showing its amazing indestructibility. We have already noted the meticulous care the Essenes took when they transcribed what came to be known as the Dead Sea Scrolls. The truth is that throughout history, faithful people have gone to great care to make sure that accurate copies of the Bible were preserved—often at great personal risk and often dedicating their lives to the laborious process.

And, by the way, after Stalin died and under the leadership of his successors, the brutal Iron Curtain from the previous century fell and millions of people under the former Communist regime were discovered to own Bibles.

Even today, a similar situation exists in China and other anti-Christian nations. Clearly, God's Word cannot be squelched.

5. Unique Structure

The remarkable structure of the Bible is yet another "selling point" in arguing its validity. Although it is a collection of 66 books, written by 40 or more different men from all walks of life over a period of 2,000 years, it is clearly one book with perfect unity and consistency throughout. At the time of their writing, the individual writers had no idea that their messages would eventually be incorporated into such a book, yet each of their works fits perfectly into place and serves its own unique purpose as a component of the whole.

6. Universal Influence

The Bible has impacted world events unlike any other document in human history. In fact, the Bible is the foundational document of Western civilization. The world's great legal documents are inspired by and quote the Bible more so than any other book. Of the world's most famous paintings, 117 depict biblical figures. The Scriptures have inspired more of the world's greatest music than all the other renowned books combined. Many of the greatest works of Bach, Brahms, Beethoven,

Mozart, Haydn, Mendelssohn and Handel reflect musical creativity that was stirred by biblical truth.

As Americans, we don't have to look far to detect the influence of the Bible and biblical ideas on our nation. Though some revisionist histories like to make much of the Deism of Jefferson, an honest reading of Jefferson's work can leave no doubt that even he was profoundly influenced by the Bible. And Jefferson was likely the least religious of the Founding Fathers, many of whom were ordained ministers of the gospel, and in whose minds and hearts the words and ideas of Scripture rang clearly. Indeed, many of the individual colonies were founded with charters that quote the Bible. Those that do not quote the Bible directly do make a direct reference to God or "Providence," and these references are made in an age and place where any reference to God or "Divine Providence" could mean nothing other than the God of the Bible. Entire educational systems were built upon biblical techniques and morals, as were the modern medical and nursing fields. The list goes on and on of the Word's profound influence on culture.

7. Life-Changing Effect

No other book besides the Bible has had such impact on humans. No other work has divided and united nations while changing the very souls of people. Shakespeare, Chopin and Spielberg could only dream of moving people like the Bible has. It is matchless, an all-time best-seller that appeals both to hearts and minds, and is beloved by at least some in every race, nation or tribe to which it has gone. Rich or poor, scholar or simpleton, king or commoner . . . the Bible has affected literally every background and walk of life. No other book has ever held such universal appeal or stirred such permanent interest.

Yet beyond its reach or appeal lies an even greater element that makes the Bible unparalleled: its lasting effect.

The testimonies of millions whose lives have been changed by the Word of God are proof enough of its profound reality. Multitudes of people, past and present, have found from personal experience that its promises are true, that its counsel is sound, that its commands and restrictions are wise and that its wonderful message of salvation meets every need for both time and eternity.

The Bible is beyond compare. As God's written Word—the recorded communication from Deity to man—it is the true supplier, nourisher and sustainer for those who believe. King David described it as "sweeter than honey to my mouth" (Ps. 119:103) and a "lamp to my feet and a light for my path" (119:105). It is indeed all that and more. And thankfully, it is not just another book whose reliability and origins are questionable. The Bible, above all other books, is as authentic as life itself.

Summary Response

Reasons confirming the Bible's
trustworthiness:

Internally consistent
Externally validated
Miraculously preserved
Comprehensively accurate
Christologically affirmed

The Bible Is Not Completely Accurate

Common Objection:
"What about all those errors in the Bible?"

Not long ago I was in Virginia when a philosophy student from the University of Virginia came up to me after a speaking engagement and introduced himself. After a bit of small talk about our common Virginia ties, he challenged me with the familiar question: "Alex, how can you possibly believe a book that's full of errors?"

I immediately asked him which error he was talking about. Somewhat taken aback by my question, he thought about it for a while and responded, "Well, everybody knows the Bible has errors. You know, being so old and all . . . it has to."

Again, I asked him which error he was referring to. After an even longer pause, he was unable to produce one. The truth was, he was merely echoing an assumption he'd heard.

As I stated in the last chapter, antiquity does not automatically imply error. The age of the Bible and its content are two completely different things. We've already proven that the Bible stands as more trustworthy than the most accepted of ancient texts. Now let's dig into the content of the Bible. Is it completely true?

I'll admit that the Bible can be a complicated book at times. There are extremely difficult passages that require a second and third look to understand. Some parts even take years of study to fully understand. But mark my words: You will never find a verifiable, proven error in Scripture. Not once.

How can I be so sure? That's exactly what this chapter is about as we examine some of the most common "sore spots" in Scripture—those elements that seem to be incorrect, incoherent or simply impossible.

"[The Bible has] God for its author, truth for its content, without any mixture of error."
—*Introduction to the 1611 King James Bible*

You Can't Make This Stuff Up!

Sadly, many potential believers use the myth that the Bible contains errors as an excuse to opt out of believing in God. Those familiar with biblical history argue that since the books of the New Testament weren't decided upon until the Council of Nicea in A.D. 327, the New Testament could have been fabricated or arbitrarily written. The assumption behind this argument is that the Early Church was uncertain as to what was and wasn't Scripture. As a result, anything and everything was fair game to be considered "Scripture." And from this, Christians made up their own religious doctrine and claimed it as God's ordained way.

The truth is that the New Testament was written long before a group of religious men sat around a table and put their stamp of approval on God's Word. The Early Church already acknowledged the same 27 books you find in your New Testament today. In A.D. 95, John finished writing the final book of the New Testament, Revelation. By around A.D. 150, Tatian wrote a commentary for the Early Church—the Diatessaron—in which he translated the four Gospels. The Syriac version and Latin translation of the New Testament, both compiled around the same time—more than 125 years before the Council of Nicea—also contain Matthew, Mark, Luke and John.

The Church did wrestle with doctrinal differences, but it is important to understand the nature of these differences. In the United States today, we're used to seeing a dozen churches on each block, each having split from the next over such "vital" issues as carpet color, using crackers for Communion rather than bread, reading from the *King James Version* or singing from hymnals rather than PowerPoint. But 2,000 years ago, Christians agreed upon the essential beliefs related to salvation by grace through faith in Jesus. They held a unified stance on this point. With the exception of various End Times views, which involved speculations about the future that could be neither proven nor disproven, the Early Church was truly united.

In other words, doctrines weren't invented or arbitrarily hashed out by individuals or groups fighting for power. What was at issue was not the doctrine itself but the best way to express it so that it would not be misinterpreted and lead to error. Christian leaders didn't defend specific doctrines for control. They defended doctrines because they believed that they were true and an essential part of the salvation message. (For proof of this, look no further than Justin's "Apology," which was written in Rome about the year A.D. 140 and speaks of the system of doctrine accepted by all known believers of the day.)

Choose Your Own Meaning

What does all this have to do with the specific "errors" of the Bible that we'll discuss in this chapter? Allow me to explain. In traveling around the country speaking to people about why Christians believe what they believe, I've noticed something: People have a strange way of reaching for *anything* when they've decided what they don't want to accept as truth. Whether it's discounting the Bible's accuracy, truthfulness or simply contending that all of Christianity is a hoax, skeptics will always find a way to rationalize their disbelief.

Unfortunately, this is just as true among Christians as it is with the greatest of doubters. The prevailing view that's leaked into the faith of many believers is simply this: *The Bible means a lot of things to lots of different people; therefore you can twist the Bible to mean anything you want it to. After all, what's true for you may not be true for me.*

It's a case of relativism and selective interpretation—choosing your own version of God's Word to fit your lifestyle. Read only the good promises, skip the "do nots" and all those miserable stories about suffering in the name of Jesus. And while you're at it, why not shape the feel-good kind of God who's sure to always provide those nice spiritual goose bumps?

Excuse me for my sarcasm, but I cringe at the thought of this emerging choose-your-own-truth version of Christianity. God is truth, and therefore His Word is truth. The Bible's content isn't up for negotiation. If you believe it is the Word of God, then you inherently acknowledge it to be the authority on life matters.

It's exactly here, at this point, where many people choose to walk away. Because for some, the notion that the Bible really is God's communicated Word—that every word is inspired—is simply too hard to swallow. So let's take a look at what gives so many people problems when it comes to the Bible's authority.

"In these fundamental truths, there are absolutely no contradictions. The so-called variations in the narratives are only the details which were most vividly impressed on one mind or another of the witnesses."

—Wilbur Smith, renowned New Testament scholar[1]

What the Bible Claims About Itself

Call it braggadocio. Call it confidence. Whatever you label the Bible's self-descriptions, they are undeniably large in every sense of the word. Psalm 119:160 defines the Bible as truth: "The entirety of Your word is truth, and every one of Your righteous judgments endures forever." The words of 2 Timothy 3:16 clearly display the Bible's claim to be inspired, meaning it was written by God Himself: "All Scripture is God-breathed and is useful for teaching, rebuking, correcting and training in righteousness" (*NIV*).

Jesus made the same claim for the Bible, saying the "Scripture cannot be broken" (John 10:35) and promising that "not the smallest letter, not the least stroke of a pen, will by any means disappear from the Law until everything is accomplished" (Matt. 5:18, *NIV*). In other words, Jesus fully believed that the Bible was God-inspired and, therefore, could not be changed or edited by mere humans. This permanence is reflected again in 1 Peter 1:25, which adds that the "word of the Lord stands forever" (*NIV*). Clearly, the Bible understands itself to be nothing less than the inspired Word of God.

Crazy Writers?

By this point, some people are already tripped up. How can a book purport to be the ultimate truth? The situation gets stickier when you include discussion of this book's writers—all of whom openly acknowledged the divine touch they were receiving as they wrote. In his writings, King David claimed, "the Spirit of the Lord spoke through me; his word was on my tongue" (2 Sam. 23:2, *NIV*). The prophet Isaiah followed many of his warnings to Israel with the phrase, "For the mouth of the Lord has spoken." And both he and fellow prophet Jeremiah wrote about God saying to them, "I have put My words in your mouth" (Isa. 51:16; Jer. 1:9). The Old Testament writers understood that they were reiterating not their words but God's words.

What about the New Testament? Luke begins his book by saying he received "perfect understanding" regarding the events that took place (1:3). The apostle Paul declares in 1 Corinthians 2 that his speech is the "demonstration of the Spirit and of power" and the "wisdom of God" (vv. 4,7). He explains that what he says is "not in words which man's wisdom teaches but which the Holy Spirit teaches" (v. 13). And as quoted earlier, Paul states in a separate letter to Timothy that "All Scripture is God-breathed and is useful for teaching, rebuking, correcting and training in righteousness" (*NIV*). The Greek word used there for "God-breathed" is reminiscent of the Old Testament prophets and means "from the mouth of God." In fact, Jesus used the same word and phrase in Matthew 4:4 when He said that man should live by "every word that proceeds from the mouth of God."

It's one thing to say you're writing a great book and predict it will become a best seller. It's an entirely different matter to claim that what you're writing is in fact the words of God Himself, that the words you're penning are infallible and authoritative to the highest degree. Yet that's exactly how the men who wrote both the Old and New Testaments felt—and they weren't shy about expressing that. Think about it: This is an astounding thing for a writer to say. If the 40-plus men who wrote the Scriptures were wrong in these claims, then they must have been either lying or insane—or both. And if this, the greatest and most influential book of the ages, containing the most beautiful literature and the most perfect moral code ever devised, was written by deceiving fanatics, then what hope is there for ever finding meaning and purpose in this world?

Fortunately, this isn't the case. We've already discussed the physical evidence behind the Bible truly being the Word of God. But there's also proof throughout the Bible itself. Biblical writers use phrases such as "Thus saith the Lord" or "The word of the Lord came to me saying . . ." at least 600 times. In total, there are around 3,000 references of the Bible as a whole, or at least a part of it, as being the Word of God. Keep in mind that none of the writers collaborated on their works. This wasn't a Bible Boys Club where everyone brainstormed book ideas. There were years—sometimes centuries—between writers. Yet it's obvious that each scribe understood the divine inspiration behind other books. The New Testament directly quotes the Old Testament more than 320 times and alludes to it more than 300 times. Even the book of Genesis, which is one of the most maligned books among critics of the Bible, is quoted in the New Testament more than 60 times. Clearly, the writers assumed that the writings were of divine origin and were, in fact, of absolute authority. This wasn't just true for them but also for the Jewish culture at large, which accepted the books as God's Word.

Again, just because a book says it is the Word of God doesn't make it so. In our day, any number of writers have made claims to "channel" God or some transcendental spirit. But, as we discussed in the previous chapter, the Bible makes claims that are specific and verifiable. The Bible makes claims that from our vantage point in time are easy to prove or disprove. And they are all true! So you have to ask yourself: If every other claim the Bible makes is true, what is my basis for saying that this claim— a claim that it makes over and over again—is false?

If you ask me, it doesn't take so much faith to believe that the Bible is the Word of God. In fact, given all of this, it would require a much larger leap of faith to *not* believe that the Bible is the Word of God!

Prone to Err . . . I Doubt It

Now that we've established that the Bible wasn't written by a bunch of crazy kooks, it's time we delve into some of the most common reasons I've heard that try to show that the Bible is full of mistakes—and how I answer them.

Where Did Cain Find His Wife?

"We don't even know her name," writes creationist researcher Ken Ham, "yet she was discussed at the 1925 Scopes trial, mentioned in the movie *Inherit the Wind*, in the book and movie *Contact*, and has been talked about in countries all over the world for hundreds of years. Is she the most-talked-about wife in history?"[2]

Skeptics have often raised the subject of Cain's wife (see Gen. 4:1–5:5) in an attempt to cast doubt on the believability of the Bible. They argue that other races of people must have existed on Earth—people not descended from Adam and Eve—in order for Cain to find a wife.

But this argument rejects the most obvious answer: that Cain married his sister. When this answer is given, those same skeptics often say, "But doesn't that violate the biblical command against incest?" The answer is an equally simple and obvious no. The command from Moses not to marry a close relation did not come until at least 400 years later (see Lev. 18–20).

It is interesting that some of the same skeptics who reject the truth of the Bible also, usually, take pride in their open-mindedness and their commitment to simple, observable facts. Yet some of these same people want to impose their modern thinking on these biblical stories. Sociologists have a name for that tendency: cultural imperialism! In other words, these skeptics who reject standards and notions of morality balk at the idea of Cain marrying a "relation" (one of his sisters)! But in reality, *all* married people ultimately marry a relation, due to the fact that humans are all descended from two common ancestors (Adam and Eve). Both the biblical text and Jewish history assert that Adam and Eve had many children. Though all males and females were ultimately related, the pool of marriageable people would have nevertheless been significant. Add to this, in these early years of human history, genetic defects that so often manifest themselves today would have then been nonexistent.

Could Jonah Really Have Survived in the Belly of a Whale?

Few biblical texts have been denied (and even ridiculed) like the story of Jonah. Forget modern reality TV shows; Jonah, having been swallowed, spit up, yet saved, was history's original *survivor*.

Skeptics of the Bible say that this could never have happened, that the story is nothing more than ancient Jewish mythology. *Three days and nights in a fish's belly? C'mon.* And it is true that the Bible does contain allegories and parables that are symbolic in nature. But Jonah exhibits a literary style befitting a historical account, not myth, parable or allegory. Jesus Himself certainly took the story to be literally true. In Matthew 12 and Luke 11, Jesus quotes from Jonah as if it were pure history. Second Kings 14:25 lists Jonah as an actual Jewish prophet. We have no record that any ancient Jews or Early Christians understood Jonah in anything other than a literal sense.

Jonah 1:17 tells us that the temporarily disobedient preacher was swallowed by a "great fish" prepared by God. In modern times, there have been several different reports of mariners who had been swallowed by whales yet survived the ordeal. It's been documented that there would have been adequate oxygen within the whale's body for a human to survive for the necessary time period. Regardless, Jonah's preservation within the body of the fish was miraculous, as was the creature's unique bout of nausea. Jonah 2:10 shows that God miraculously caused the prophet's ejection from the creature.

Remember, if God had power to create the universe, our solar system and planet Earth, then there is no reason to suppose that He could not intervene within the created order. In other words, *miraculous acts of God are logically possible.* While both the fish's swallowing and Jonah's survival require miraculous intervention, such things would pose no problem to an all-powerful God. Objections against the story of Jonah (the last miracle recorded in the Old Testament) come not from textual or logical problems, but from an anti-supernatural bias—a predisposition against miraculous occurrences.

Incidentally, the "fish story" isn't the only miraculous element in the story of Jonah. Jonah contains accounts of God's most significant activity within the finite world: the miracle of *conversion.* Jonah 3:5-10 tells us that the sinful people of Ninevah indeed turned to God. Jesus later pointed to Ninevah's conversion as a spiritual benchmark for listeners of His own day to consider (see Matt. 12:41). Again, Jesus spoke of both Jonah and Ninevah in terms of history, not mythology.

When Did the Census of Luke 2 Really Take Place?

Some have questioned the Bible's claim that a census or registration took place under Rome's Caesar Augustus. The controversy surrounds the date of the census that Luke 2:2 says coincided with the birth of Jesus. In *Antiquities,* Jewish historian Josephus reports a census by governor Quirinius that would have taken place about A.D. 6. But Luke's account says that a census (during the administration of Quirinius) coincided with Christ's birth. What gives?

Discovery of a Latin inscription in 1764 strongly indicates that Quirinius was in power during *two different time periods*. Quirinius had extensive military experience and leadership skills, having overcome an uprising against Rome by the Homonadensians between 12 and 2 B.C.[3] Roman emperor Caesar Augustus (who lived until A.D. 14), thus, apparently placed Quirinius in power on two separate occasions. The wording of Luke 2:2 also seems to indicate that Quirinius led more than one administration over the province. One objective for Caesar's taxations/enrollments was to keep records for military purposes. Jews were not required to serve in the Roman army, but payment of taxes was unavoidable. It is known that a census took place around 4 B.C., and it was during this time that travel to Bethlehem would have been necessary for Joseph.

Don't the Biblical Accounts of Easter Morning Conflict?

Some say the New Testament gives conflicting information about Jesus' resurrection and the empty tomb. Skepticism about the resurrection ranges from those who question the Gospels' accuracy or precision with the details all the way to some who say that Early Church leaders actively lied and purposely provided misleading information. Here's a look at the variances:

Keep in mind that no individual Gospel writer gives *every* detail about what happened. But all convey the core facts. In no way does it logically follow that a partial account is a false account. The key facts regarding Christ's death and resurrection are agreed upon by all four Gospels: (1) that Jesus was dead and buried; (2) that the disciples were devastated by this; (3) that in fear and despair, they scattered; (4) that on the third day, the stone had been removed; (5) that the tomb was found empty; (6) that angels appeared and conveyed a message; (7) that Jesus had risen; (8) that Jesus appeared to His disciples; and (9) that all of the disciples eventually accepted His resurrection as conclusive.

MATTHEW 28	MARK 16
Time that the empty tomb was discovered:	
"As the first day of the week began to dawn" (v. 1)	"Early in the morning, on the first day of the week . . . when the sun had risen" (v. 2)
Who:	
"Mary Magdalene and the other Mary" (v. 1)	"Mary Magdalene, Mary the mother of James, and Salome" (v. 1)
Status of the stone that had sealed the tomb:	
"rolled back the stone from the door" (v. 2)	"the stone had been rolled away" (v. 4)
Information on the angels:	
"angel of the Lord" (v. 2)	"entering into the tomb, they saw a young man clothed in a long white robe sitting on the right side" (v. 5)
Angel's message:	
"Do not be afraid, for I know that you seek Jesus who was crucified. He is not here; for He is risen, as He said. Come, see the place where the Lord lay. And go quickly and tell His disciples that He is risen from the dead, and indeed He is going before you into Galilee; there you will see Him. Behold, I have told you" (vv. 5-7)	"Do not be alarmed. You seek Jesus of Nazareth, who was crucified. He is risen! He is not here. See the place where they laid Him. But go, tell His disciples—and Peter—that He is going before you into Galilee; there you will see Him, as He said to you" (vv. 6-7; the Greek of Mark 16:6-7 is virtually identical with that of Matthew 28)

LUKE 24	JOHN 20
Time that the empty tomb was discovered:	
"On the first day of the week, very early in the morning" (v. 1)	"The first day of the week . . . while it was still dark" (v. 1)
Who:	
"they . . ." (v. 1)	"Mary Magdalene" (v. 1)
Status of the stone that had sealed the tomb:	
"they found the stone rolled away . . . they went in" (vv. 2-3)	". . . and saw that the stone had been taken away" (v. 1)
Information on the angels:	
"two men stood by them in shining garments" (v. 4)	
Angel's message:	
"Why do you seek the living among the dead? He is not here, but is risen! Remember how He spoke to you when He was still in Galilee, saying, 'The Son of Man must be delivered into the hands of sinful men, and be crucified, and the third day rise again'" (vv. 5-7)	

Just as journalists who each cover the same story may report different details, the Gospel reporters emphasize unique aspects about Christ's resurrection. If each account were identical, skeptics would surely fault the Gospel writers for having written in collusion. Had that been the case, Matthew, Mark, Luke and John could have simply signed their four names at the bottom of one account. In a court of law, differing details within agreement on a main point not only add validity but also credibility.

"One is often surprised to find how many apparent contradictions [in the Gospel resurrection accounts] turn out not to be contradictory at all, but merely supplementary. . . . Divergences appear very great on first sight . . . But the fact remains that all of [the resurrection accounts], without exception, can be made to fall into a place in a single orderly and coherent narrative, without the smallest contradiction or difficulty and without any suppression, invention, or manipulation, beyond a trifling effort to imagine the natural behavior of a bunch of startled people running about in the dawn-light between Jerusalem and the garden."

—Dr. Dorothy Sayers, scholar, essayist and playwright[4]

Remember that no details given in one Gospel contradict a detail given in another Gospel. The small details are all pieces that complete the big picture. Some may ask, "But what about the time of day that people arrived at the tomb? Matthew says it was 'dawn,' Mark speaks of the 'rising of the sun.' Luke just says it was 'early,' and the Gospel of John says, 'yet dark.'" In reality, the journey from Bethany to Jerusalem is some three to five miles. The walk would have easily taken long enough for the sky to go from darkness to daylight.

Others have inquired about the number of women who were present at Jesus' vacant tomb that first Easter morning. Matthew and Mark both speak of the two Marys, yet Mark also mentions Salome. Luke refers to the people at the tomb as "they," while John only names Mary Magdalene. What are we to make of this crowd who apparently may or may not have been at Jesus' tomb?

It's important to note that none of the Gospels say that *only* Mary Magdalene went to the tomb. Luke 24:2 uses the collective "they." He also mentions "Joanna . . . and the other women" (24:10). Mention of *one* person by a certain Gospel writer does not automatically rule out the possible inclusion of other persons.

Finally, let's consider the number of angels at the empty tomb. Matthew and Mark mention one angel, yet Luke and John mention two. But remember, Matthew and Mark never say only one angel appeared. No writer says that only one angel spoke. Each Gospel gives a distinct perspective, mentioning unique—though certainly not contradictory—details.

It's amazing to me how critics of the Bible will use any tactic to take jabs at the book's validity. Some arguments are understandable, given certain passages' difficult and often cryptic meanings. Some attacks are simply ludicrous and birthed out of spite. But at the end of the day, *all* are eventually empty claims. God did not write a book full of mistakes. His Word is not error-prone. Whether that's established through plain logic or years of investigation, it remains the undeniable truth.

Summary Response

Reasons to accept that the Bible is accurate,
understandable and intelligible:

The Reason of Truth
*The specific, verifiable claims of Scripture have
all been found to be true.*

The Testimony of the Church
*The Church throughout history—even during the
first century, when there were eyewitnesses still alive to
many of the incidents recorded in Scripture—
took Scripture to be true.*

The Results of Orthodoxy
*The teachings of Scripture have had a tremendous
impact on individuals and culture. Its impact and power
are not just slightly greater than other books
but are of a different species altogether.*

Jesus Was Just a Man

Common Question:
"What makes Jesus so different from
other great men of history?"

No figure in history has been surrounded by more controversy than Jesus Christ. Before His arrival on Earth, people debated how this Savior of the Jewish people would come take His throne and, as God's Son, restore Israel to its former glory. During His life, He was maligned for being a complete fraud, for blaspheming by claiming to be God's Chosen One, and for conjuring up magical "miracles" to convince the weak-minded of His authenticity. And after His death . . . well, you don't have to look far to find arguments that He in fact never existed.

So who was Jesus, if He indeed walked the face of this earth? I believe that the labels both skeptics and believers use in their attempts to define Jesus fit into five general categories. And in discussing Jesus, it's essential that we come to a logical conclusion as to which one of these we find true so that we can base all our subsequent findings on that foundation. Let's look at the five different views and decide.

1. *Myth.* This view, popularized by British philosopher/logician Bertrand Russell and by publications such as *The Skeptical Inquirer*, claims that Jesus was simply an element of folklore. As a legendary, fictitious character, His life was made up by a lower-class

culture as an emblem of hope and was passed along through misguided generations, who then further distorted the story.

2. *Man.* Accepting the notion that Jesus did in fact exist, this view claims He was simply a human with serious psychological issues and a massive God-complex. From our modern vantage point, and with the tools of history, science and journalism, we know of many such people—from passionate political ideologues to cult leaders. Social scientists and others have identified many cases of charismatic leaders who have been able to induce a kind of mass hypnosis on their followers, and this view holds that Jesus had similar incredible powers of persuasion. He was able to brainwash His disciples by His charismatic and convincing demeanor. This view holds that His followers simply misunderstood who Jesus really was and wrote their New Testament books in error. Or maybe Jesus had misunderstandings about Himself.

3. *Mystic.* Is it possible that Jesus was someone between a myth and a man—that He did indeed have strange powers derived by fully channeling His internal being? Some New Age followers hold Him up as an esoteric guru. They note that much of Jesus' life is unrecorded in Scripture. They claim that these unrecorded years—"the lost years of Jesus"—were devoted to journeys to India or elsewhere to learn how to direct His mental and metaphysical energy. This view holds that the uneducated followers of Jesus were overwhelmed by these displays of power

and therefore called Him "God" and were enamored by His "miracles."

4. *Misrepresentation.* Some believe Jesus is the result of a powerful undercover ploy by the Church to control people. After all, the corruption of the Church is well documented throughout history; how far-fetched is it to believe that manipulative Church leaders concocted the Jesus story to sway naive believers. Maybe Jesus was posthumously deified and was in fact a simple man given God-like status by carefully devised tall tales. Christian doctrine, then, is not the product of *divine* revelation but of *human* speculation. And since the motivation behind it is beyond sketchy, it's safe to say the religion is nothing more than a blown-up cult—a dangerous, irrelevant convergence of hype surrounding a misrepresented man.

5. *Messiah.* Or was Jesus actually the Messiah? That's the money question that this chapter is all about. Because as long as Jesus is considered just another human being, it's impossible to make sense of His mysterious life and death. But once His divinity is established and accepted, everything changes. For one thing, if Jesus is indeed God in human form, then all of His miracles can be explained by His power. But—and more to the point here—if Jesus is indeed God, then we have a choice to make: to follow Him or not. To accept His claim to be "the way, the truth, and the life"—or not.

As you can easily see, much rides on the question! Fortunately for believers, proving His uniqueness as God's Son isn't a crapshoot. As my friend Josh McDowell so poignantly and famously wrote—in fact, it became the title of his most famous book—there is "evidence that demands a verdict."

Elements of a God

If you've read this far in this book, it should come as no surprise to you when I say that I believe Jesus to be the Messiah. So the question before us now is this: On what grounds do I draw this conclusion? Though there are many ways to go about answering this question, I will focus on five areas. Jesus stands out above all people by virtue of these five distinct characteristics or qualities of His life:

1. His prophesied coming
2. His supernatural birth
3. His miraculous deeds
4. His distinctive teaching
5. His confirmatory actions

Stated another way, we can generally say that Jesus was unique by who He was, what He did, what He claimed about Himself (and heaven), and what He did to substantiate those claims. Anyone can waltz into a crowded room and announce that he's just arrived from the planet Xanthos. (Try this and see what kind of reaction you'll get.) For people to take you seriously, though, you have to prove it. You have to know what the planet's surface looks like, what life forms exist on the planet, how you got there and back, where this planet is, and so forth. But most of all, you have to have physical, undeniable proof. Our tendency as humans isn't to believe sight unseen—we like evidence. And for most of us, there's no better evidence than tangible, visual evidence.

"I know of no one fact in the history of mankind which is proved by better, fuller evidence of every sort than the great sign that Christ died and rose again from the dead."
—*Thomas Arnold, professor of history at Rugby University in Oxford, England*[1]

It All Hinges On . . .

The greatest proof of Jesus' uniqueness is His physical resurrection.

Jesus Himself intended us to accept or reject who He claimed to be, and what He taught, based on the resurrection. During His lifetime, He predicted His death and resurrection—including a final prediction the night before His death. Though Jesus had performed many miracles—including the raising of people from the dead—His own physical resurrection was His way of proving that what He had said and who He claimed to be were true.

So, obviously, the truth of the resurrection is a central question. And, just as obviously, anyone wanting to disprove Christianity would have to discredit the historicity of this event. Put simply, either the resurrection happened and Jesus is who He claimed to be, or it didn't and we are under no obligation to any of His teachings or example. We can—and should!—do as we please.

That is also why no event in history has been shrouded with more speculation, skepticism and relentless examination than the hours of Christ's death and the discovery of His empty tomb. For both Christians and nonbelievers, it is the crux of all history. Why so dramatically wide-sweeping? Because for those who believe in Jesus and His resurrection, it is potentially the wonderful gateway into an everlasting life. But for those who reject the notion, it is possibly the one-way ticket to an eternity of unimaginable misery.

I don't know about you, but that sounds like a pretty big deal to me.

The apostle Paul fully understood the magnitude of what the resurrection entails to both believers and nonbelievers. In 1 Corinthians 15:14, he wrote, "If Christ be not risen, then our preaching is vain, and your faith is also vain" (*KJ21*). He clearly points out the negative consequences if Jesus *hadn't* risen from the dead. He goes on to conclude that if Christ didn't have the power to overcome death, and if our faith is nothing more than empty, false hope, then we're still bound to our permanent state of sin (see v. 17). Not only that, but our loved ones who we thought were in heaven are not (see v. 18) . . . *and*—as Paul says oh-so-gingerly—we hopeless Christians are the most miserable people in the world (see v. 19)! That's pretty sad.

Obviously, Christ's resurrection is of paramount importance because it confirms both the *man* and His *message*. Thankfully, as always, God has not left us believers out in the cold. He knew we would want proof, which is why Acts 1:3 says, "He also presented Himself alive after His suffering by many infallible proofs." The word "proofs" in this verse, *tekmerion,* is a form of the Greek root word *tekmar* and means "a criterion of certainty" or "a certain, infallible proof."[2] It's from this word that we derive our English word "technical." This particular term is found only once in the Bible (in Acts 1:3) and means "the highest level of proof." In other words, it was known to those of Jesus' day—with undeniable certainty—that He had come back from the dead.

But can we know with undeniable certainty today?

"No intelligent jury in the world could fail to bring in a verdict that indeed the resurrection story is true."

—Lord Darling, former chief justice of England[3]

Knowing a Fake When You See One

Before we divulge the actual proof of Jesus rising from the dead, I want to present a few of the main theories *against* His resurrection. I do this not to try your patience—don't we all just want to cut to the chase as quickly as possible?—but to thoroughly examine both sides of the coin. You've probably heard the analogy of how the U.S. government discovers counterfeit money, but it perfectly underscores the approach to establishing whether Christ's resurrection is legit or not.

When the U.S. Treasury trains people to find fake bills, they don't show them catalogues full of forged replicas of $1, $5, $20, $50 and $100 bills. Instead, a trainee spends hours upon hours of studying the *real* thing. He knows how each authentic bill is cut, what it smells like, what its exact texture is, how it wrinkles, folds and crimps, where its ridges are—everything about it. Essentially, he knows the real deal inside and out, backward and forward. So when this examiner is handling thousands of bills within a time frame, he can quickly discern the fake from the real not by what a bill *is* but by what it *isn't*.

We would do well to take the same approach to history's greatest event. As we examine the arguments against Jesus' rise from the dead, we can quickly determine whether they contain any merit by a standard used by both believers and doubters: logic. Though many find this idea hard to accept, the resurrection can be proven by rational, cogent and sound evidence.

Think again about the implications of what we're dealing with. If Jesus really had power over death, then He had a staggering level of ability. Jesus seemed to have powers that belong only to God—namely control over life and death. Not only could we not bring ourselves back from the dead, be we also don't have the power to *will* our own death. Remember, Jesus willfully caused the cessation of His bodily functions, that is,

He *chose* (willed) the moment of His physical death (see Matt. 27:50; Mark 15:37; Luke 23:46; John 19:30).

Though He was nailed to the cross, it was not the crucifixion that ultimately took Jesus' life from Him. Luke 23:46 says that Jesus "dismissed His spirit." Obviously, you and I couldn't do that. Sure, people can commit suicide and end their life by using some external means. But Jesus, with power over life, willed the cessation of involuntary functions and initiated the separation of body and soul. This is a power belonging only to God.

In addition, Jesus had (and exercised) the ability to bring Himself back from the dead—that is, He arose from the grave. For a moment, forget about Jesus' prophesied coming, virgin birth, sinless nature, unique teaching, loving example, miraculous deeds and perfect life. His uniqueness and deity is confirmed by these two facts alone: He exerted control over life and had victorious power over death. No other figure in all of history can list these abilities on their résumé. Jesus stands alone.

Yet for some reason, people aren't sold that easily. Accounts of Jesus' rising from the dead haven't gone unchallenged. So let's look at the major ways that people have attempted to debunk Christ's resurrection.

1. The Fraud Theory

This theory argues that Jesus' resurrection was a hoax. Christ did not rise. The tomb was not empty. Basically, it's all a big deception. What do people use to argue this? First, they believe the women accidentally went to the wrong tomb and that their claim of Jesus' body no longer being present was simply a case of mistaking an already empty tomb for His.

Fraud theorists also have many arguments involving Jesus' body being stolen. The first four entail that either Joseph of Arimathea, the gardener, the Roman soldiers or the Jews were involved in a classic case of body snatching. Lastly, they argue that it's possible that the disciples stole the body and then lied about Christ's post-crucifixion appearances in their writings.

So how do we answer these charges? Let's take them one by one.

Examining the Evidence

There was no mistaking which tomb Christ was buried in. The resurrection of Jesus was the capstone of a week in which He was the focal point of all that was going on in Jerusalem. Today the mass media tend to blow up such events as the O. J. Simpson or Michael Jackson trials. If there were mass media in those days, they would have undoubtedly been tuned in to the events of Jesus' death, burial and resurrection. Without mass media, everyone tuned themselves in to each turn of events. There could be no confusion over who this "infamous" person was or where His body lay.

Now let's address issues surrounding the tomb itself. Jesus' tomb was likely guarded by heavily equipped Roman soldiers ready to attack any intruders to the point of death. It's possible that the guards were Jewish temple guards. The Bible is not explicit on this point. Either way, these guards and their bosses had a strong motivation for keeping the body of Jesus secure. For both the Jews and the Romans, the disappearance of the body of Jesus would create huge problems. Any mishap would call into question the Roman authorities' ability to lead, as well as the assertion of the Jewish leaders that Jesus was just an ordinary man—not the Messiah. And, on a more personal level, if the guards were Roman, failure was not an option. If anything happened to Jesus' body, it was a given that they would be held responsible and would be killed. Their very lives were at stake.

Add to this the fact that the tomb was blocked by a massive, one-and-a-half to two-ton stone—obviously, not something the disciples could have easily moved. To steal Jesus' body, the disciples would have had to overcome the guards, move the stone, break what was likely—according to many historians—a mortar seal over the tomb and remove the body. They would have to do all of this without anyone seeing or hearing the commotion it would have likely caused in the still hours of the night and early morning. When you factor in the fact that the disciples were all scattered and hiding in fear—Scripture verifies their fleeing after the night in Gethsemane—this argument verges on the ridiculous.

As for others stealing the body, the Romans had no reason for swiping Jesus' corpse—they had sentenced the man, so what would secretly removing His body accomplish except for causing the citizens to question their authority? Likewise, the Jews had no reason to take Christ's body because the last thing they wanted was rumor of a resurrection. This was the exact thing Jesus had been cryptically prophesying throughout His ministry. At the time of His death, something clicked; people began to realize what He had been predicting. The Jews would have jumped at any chance they had to disprove His now-apparent claims of overcoming death. So if indeed they had managed to steal the body, they would have loudly publicized its presence. With a body, they could have exposed Christ's heresy and instantly killed Christianity. Instead, they were left with yet another irrefutable thorn in their sides: that Jesus was no longer in the tomb.

Consider also that Jesus' followers wouldn't have broken the Sabbath. Christ's tomb was discovered empty the day following the Sabbath, meaning His disciples would have had to act the day before, on the most revered Jewish holy day. As faithful Jews themselves, it's highly doubtful to assume they would have broken not only the Sabbath laws but also Jesus' commands to adhere to honoring the Sabbath. Furthermore, they had no reason to steal the body. Think about it: They weren't expecting Him to rise, so why would they bother retrieving what they would have assumed was simply a corpse?

But Wait, There's More

Those are all solid arguments that unravel the logic behind the Fraud Theory. There are additional—and still logic-based—ones that completely dismantle it. First, it's important for us to understand that liars don't make martyrs.

You could argue, for example, that the 9/11 terrorists were liars, or at least seriously mistaken. We might say, and even be able to demonstrate, that what they believed was and is false, even though they believed it was true.

Of course, you could also say that the first-century martyrs were mistaken or deluded as well. But if you make that argument, you have to disregard the most crucial point of this chapter, a point so crucial that we started the chapter with it and have returned to it repeatedly. And that fact is the physical resurrection of Jesus. The Christian martyrs of the first century did not die for an idea or a promise. They died because they were eyewitnesses to the resurrected Jesus. If Jesus' body was stolen (which we've already shown as not only unlikely but impossible), then the disciples would have all eventually died for something they *knew* was not true. With the exception of John, the disciples each endured horrific deaths. They were variously crucified, boiled in a vat, and subject to other tortures and horrific ends. No sane person would willingly go through such torment simply to publicly "validate" a lie he had concocted.

So were the early followers of Jesus insane? Deluded? An honest assessment must consider the possibility. But an honest assessment must also consider this: Everything else we know about Jesus' early followers strongly suggests that they were not crazy. They wrote, they traveled, they spoke to small groups and large and they otherwise behaved in ways that showed an extreme clarity of mind.

"It was therefore impossible that [the disciples] could have per-sisted in affirming the truths they have narrated, had not Jesus actually risen from the dead, and had they not known this fact as certainly as they knew any other fact . . . The resurrection of Christ is the most verifiable fact of ancient history."

—Simon Greenleaf, founder of Harvard School of Law, after thorough investigation of whether or not Christ rose from the dead[4]

No, the early disciples of Jesus were sane—but they were somehow transformed. In a matter of days, these cowards became fearless men, willing to die for the sake of what they'd seen. In fact, one of the disciples, Peter, is said to have been crucified upside-down at his own request, because he did not consider himself to be worthy of crucifixion in the same way Jesus was crucified!

How do we account for such physical and moral courage if the body was stolen? Not a single disciple ever changed his story. Each was willing to die for the truth that Jesus, the Son of God and Savior of the world, actually lived, died and rose again. Their lives, and the manner of their deaths, are powerful testimonies to the truth of the claims of Jesus.

Finally, we must bear in mind one obvious question: If this was indeed a fraud set up by the disciples (or whoever else the-orists blame), how can we explain the numerous appearances of Jesus after His death? Christ didn't just appear to His disciples; He was seen on different occasions by Paul, James, a small group of people . . . even 500 "brethren" at once (see sidebar). Can you imagine trying to convince 500 people to all tell the same lie? To account for this, some additional—and far-reaching—theory would have to be tacked on.

The Recorded Resurrection Appearances of Jesus

To Mary Magdalene (see John 20:11)
To "the other" women (see Matt. 28:9-10)
To Peter (see Luke 24:34)
To two disciples (see Luke 24:13-32)
To 10 apostles (see Luke 24:33-49)
To Thomas and the other apostles (see John 20:26-30)
To seven apostles (see John 21:1-23)
To *all* the apostles (see Matt. 28:16-20)
To all the apostles again (see Acts 1:4-9)
To 500 brethren at once (see 1 Cor. 15:6)
To James (see 1 Cor. 15:7)
To Paul (see 1 Cor. 15:7)

---

2. The Swoon Theory

A second line of argument to refute Jesus' resurrection contends that Christ was never actually dead after all. This theory claims that life never left His body on the cross, and that somehow in the cold, dank tomb, He revived. It also makes the assumption that He moved the one-and-a-half to two-ton stone from the grave entrance; either snuck by the armed and extremely fit (and capable) Roman guards—who would lose their lives, mind you, if anything went wrong—or overcame these soldiers, despite being wounded, bloody and dehydrated to the point of collapsing; and then traveled across Jerusalem incognito, despite being the talk of the town, with the entire city knowing who He was, what He'd done and where He was.

Once Jesus had located and regrouped His followers, this theory continues, He convinced them all that He had defeated death and had come through with His own promise. (It's also assumed that the disciples never once connected the dots between Christ's poor physical condition—following the argument that He in fact never died—and His supposed resurrection.) Unaware that they'd been deceived, these disciples then went out and gave their lives for this "gospel."

Sound ludicrous? Hey, it's not my idea. I'm not the one making this up! If you ever get into a discussion with a Swoon Theorist, here are a few things you can point out.

Even apart from the whole resurrection story, archeology confirms the gory details of crucifixion. Put plainly, it was not survivable. In fact, the very term was equivalent with the word "death" simply because *no one* survived. If a victim had not perished by suffocation while hanging on the cross, Roman guards would hasten death by breaking that person's legs, making it impossible for him to push up and breathe. In Jesus' case, Pilate sent a soldier for this specific reason, yet He was pronounced dead upon examination. Just to make sure, Jesus' side was pierced by a massive spear, which if He weren't already dead, would have surely killed Him. The heart is surrounded by a sac of water called the pericardium. Any breach of this membrane would have meant instant death. In fact, the pleural fluids that gushed out of Jesus' side were medical evidence of this. The mix of blood and water clearly proved to everyone present that day that Christ was indeed dead.

"[Jesus] couldn't possibly have faked his death, because you can't fake the inability to breathe for long. Besides, the spear thrust into his heart would have settled the issue once and for all. And the Romans weren't about to risk their own death by allowing him to walk away alive. [The Swoon Theory is] a fanciful theory without any possible basis in fact."

—Dr. Alexander Metherell, expert on the medical, archaeological, historical and biblical evidence surrounding the crucifixion and death of Christ[5]

Somehow for those who believe the Swoon Theory, that's not enough. So let's continue flattening these notions. (I don't know about you, but I'm having fun dismantling these silly arguments!) To convince those dealing with His supposedly dead body, Jesus would have had to remain *completely* motionless for several hours—no reactions, no signs of breathing, nothing. The women's preparation of His body for burial involved wrapping it head to toe in cloth and anointing it with 75 pounds worth of burial spices. That would obviously take awhile. And yet according to the Swoon Theory, Jesus was able to endure the entire process without ever once showing signs of life.

Then there's Jesus' physical condition. He had been beaten senseless and had a crown of massive thorns smashed into His scalp. Isaiah 50:6 prophesied that His beard was ripped out. There is no account of this particular brutality in the New Testament version, but neither is there any reason to doubt it. Certainly Jesus suffered tremendous indignity in the hours before His death. He'd been whipped and flogged with a skin-shredding instrument of torture (His back would have literally been filleted after His 39 lashes) and He was forced to carry a 150-pound cross across Jerusalem. Finally, His hands and feet had been nailed to the cross, and He'd had a spear thrust into His side.

Now, after all that, we're supposed to believe that He was not dead, but merely unconscious? It is simply not possible that any human could have undergone such physical brutality and been pronounced dead by the experts of his day—only to recover consciousness three days later and be physically robust enough to do all the things Jesus subsequently did. After all, even assuming that He somehow was not dead, but merely unconscious, if He did regain consciousness He would have been in extremely critical condition, totally unfit for anything but many months or even years of recovery. But the Swoon Theory says otherwise. This theory says He then moved the one-and-a-half to two-ton stone by Himself, broke a mortar seal, subdued a group of guards and trekked across town!

No, the Swoon Theory becomes more outrageous the more you examine it. The sheer physical element of Jesus' wounded condition makes this theory logically impossible to a point beyond the comical.

"Jesus' death as a consequence of crucifixion is indisputable."
—Gerd Ludemann, German New Testament scholar, who claims to be an atheist[6]

Speaking of the disciples, it's interesting how this theory tries to explain away the resurrection by placing an exceedingly high "stupidity quotient" on these 11 followers (stolen body, mistakenly going to the wrong tomb, Jesus wasn't really dead, hallucinations, and so forth.). Let's get one thing straight: The disciples were not stupid. They knew the difference between a dead man and a living one, and they'd clearly seen their teacher crucified. Sure, they may not have been as sophisticated as we like to think we were today. And yes, many of them had simple blue-collar backgrounds. But let's not forget that Luke was a physician and Matthew was an accountant of sorts. These guys were no dummies.

Finally, none of the Swoon Theory's assumptions accounts for the other instances in which Jesus appeared after being resurrected. (See the previous section for the numerous appearances recorded in Scripture.)

3. The Hallucination Theory

Though brief in its arguments against the resurrection, the Hallucination Theory is given the same credence by skeptics as other cases against Jesus rising from the dead. This one simply holds that the disciples experienced visions. They merely *thought* they saw their teacher alive again. The entire series of events was all a part of their imaginations, possibly caused by the obvious stress they were under. In fact, this theory goes so far as to say that although Jesus' subsequent resurrection appearances were numerous, happened shortly after His death and were credibly reported, these accounts *all* should be attributed to the witnesses' imaginations. People *wanted* to see Jesus alive; therefore they imagined Him alive.

Though this theory may seem *really* far-fetched to some, allow me to dissect it with the same attention we've given others. First, we must realize that there is no evidence that hallucinations are contagious. You don't share visions. Hallucinations are a largely *personal* phenomenon.

You may say, "Well, people—even groups of people—believe all kinds of wacky things. What about people who believe in UFOs or Bigfoot or the Loch Ness Monster?" That's an interesting but entirely different question. If I see something in the sky, or in the woods, or in a Scottish lake, that I cannot identify, and then I encounter other people who have seen things they can't identify, that does not prove we experienced a mass hallucination. And if two or more of us get together and come up with a common explanation for what we saw, neither does that mean that we're right.

So, hallucinations are localized and occur in the mind of one individual. Granted, attempts to explain the mysterious—even false explanations—can develop followers who could all end up being wrong. But is that what happened in the case of Jesus' resurrection? Jesus appeared to different people, at entirely different times and places. He appeared to people He knew intimately and to others who had not known Him. They all came to a common conclusion: They saw Jesus.

Add to this that illusions can't be touched, can't cook meals and can't eat food—all of which Jesus was or did. Consider the actions attributed to the resurrected Christ in passages such as Matthew 28:9-10,16-20; Mark 16:14-18; Luke 24:13-53; and John 20:11-29; 21:1-25.

Let's also consider the mental state of the disciples. Medical science tells us that hallucinations occur to people who have been deprived of food and water, who have mental problems, who are on drugs, who are expecting to see something, and so forth. The disciples fit none of these profiles. Not only that, we can't forget that they honestly didn't expect to see Jesus again! Why would they imagine something they'd already dismissed?!

Finally, in order to account for all of the known data, the Hallucination Theory requires additional input from another naturalistic theory. In other words, in order for this theory to ring true, others have to be true as well. For instance, let's assume the women mistakenly looked in the wrong tomb. That still doesn't answer why the body was never recovered. Was it stolen? Moved? Misplaced? To answer this, skeptics must rely on assumptions from another theory such as the Fraud Theory—

making the Hallucination Theory even less plausible on its own.

"As a lawyer, I have made a prolonged study of the evidences for the events of the first Easter. To me, the evidence is absolutely conclusive. Over and over in the court I have secured the verdict on evidences not nearly so compelling."
—Sir Edward Clarke, nineteenth-century English lawyer[7]

---

4. Other Anti-resurrection Theories

There are other anti-resurrection theories. Let me list a few here before I deal with their common argument:

- Jesus' resurrection was just a spiritual thing. In other words, He overcame death in the spirit, but never physically rose.
- The resurrection of Jesus is just a heart matter. Christ "lives" only in a symbolic way, inhabiting my heart and my life. It was never meant to be a physical thing.
- Jesus was either an alien or was acted upon by a group of extra-terrestrials.
- The "Christ of faith" and the "Jesus of history" are two completely different figures.
- Jesus was never crucified, but Judas was crucified, mistakenly, in Jesus' place (taught to Muslims based on an obscure verse in the Koran).

Books have been written about each of these theories—even the idea that Jesus was an alien! (In 1968, the best-selling book *Chariots of the Gods?* suggested that most of the ancient religions were actually founded by aliens who were welcomed by more primitive Earthlings as gods. Amazingly, the book became an international phenomenon, selling more than 10 million copies!) And these theories are just a scratching of the surface. It is not hard to come up with a reason for not believing something.

But I mention these theories to ask you two questions before we go on. The first question is this: If you say that the resurrection did *not* exist, how can you be sure? In the face of this historical evidence and the testimonies of eyewitnesses who appear to be credible, surely it would take a great deal of either faith or irrefutable evidence or both to prove that the resurrection did not exist. And if the evidence does not exist, then we face another interesting question: How much evidence do *you* need in order to believe? I have already presented a great deal of historical and logical evidence that points toward the reality of the resurrection—much more evidence, by the way, than exists for a very large number of ancient events that we universally accept as true. And much more evidence than exists to the contrary.

So why is it that so many people are so committed to denying the truth of the resurrection? Again, we go back to the idea that began this chapter: Everything hangs on this one event. Either it is false, and we are free to do as we please . . . or it is true, and everything Jesus claimed about Himself must be taken seriously.

With so much at stake, and with some of the more common theories about the resurrection out of the way, or at least put in their proper perspective, let's move on.

Not So Original

We often give the disciples less credit than they deserve. We've already hit on the fact that many skeptics assume in their arguments that these followers were virtual morons, unable to discern between a dead man and a living one. But the Bible points out that the disciples—yes, even they—had heard it all before. These attempts to explain away the resurrection were not anything new even during the time of the disciples. They'd caught wind of the attempts at explaining away the resurrection through supernatural-based theories, that maybe Jesus was a ghost of sorts or a great magician/con artist who had struck up a deal with a higher power.

In fact, the disciples had initially doubted themselves and had experienced many aspects of these theories. Luke 24:11-12 shows that at first they refused to believe the women who had seen Jesus, possibly chalking it up to the ladies' lack of sleep or to wishful thinking. Peter was such a skeptic, in fact, that he had to go check out the scene for himself. And when these guys finally saw Jesus face to face (see Luke 24:37)? Forget heroic notions of followers filled with powerful faith—they thought He was a ghost!

The women themselves at first were skeptical. Twice, Mary Magdalene expressed her concerns that "they" had stolen Jesus' body (see John 20:2,13). Who was she referring to? Though it's never spelled out, she was most likely talking about either Roman or Jewish authorities—both of whom were handling the entire affair.

In the end, it's crucial to realize that all of these theories—Fraud, Swoon, Hallucination—had already been considered by the disciples. Their conclusion? No theory can account for the empty tomb (see Matt. 28:6) that would forever remind them—and us—that Jesus had indeed risen from the dead.

Somebody Testify!

When it comes to making a bold statement about the verifiable truth of Jesus' resurrection, no one does it better than the apostle Paul in 1 Corinthians 15. This chapter is his "no-spin" version of what really happened, a section of his letter virtually dedicated to all the doubters and haters out there. (Can't you imagine the vigor with which Paul wrote this, as if he were a lawyer pacing the floor before an unpersuaded, disbelieving jury?)

His defense covers the gamut in recounting Jesus' purposeful death (it was no accident), His physical resurrection (death was not final) and the subsequent sightings by many people (it was no fraud). It's significant to note that this chapter contains eyewitness testimony recorded close to the times when the actual events occurred. In verses 5 to 8, he lays out a descriptive list of those who encountered a risen Jesus. By this account, we know of more than 600 people who saw the risen Jesus alive after He had been executed by crucifixion: Peter, 500 brethren at once, 120 apostles, James, Paul and the entire group of 12 disciples.

"The date, therefore, at which Paul received the fundamentals of the Gospel cannot well be later than some seven years after the death of Jesus Christ. It may be earlier."

—New Testament scholar C. H. Dodd on the timing of Paul's writing of 1 Corinthians 15[8]

We also have testimonies of Christ's resurrection from two significant converts: James and Paul. James was the earthly brother of Jesus, yet he refused to believe in his sibling's miraculous rising from the dead until he saw Christ firsthand. When he did, he could not deny the absolute truth that he'd personally witnessed. Paul, on the other hand, is probably the Bible's greatest account of redemption. Initially known as Saul, he was the chief of Christian-haters. He loathed Christians so much that his job was to track them down and have them persecuted. He was feared by all who confessed Jesus as their Lord. (Talk about not having psychological preconditions for hallucination!)

Yet one face-to-face meeting with Jesus changed every facet of this man's life. After being struck blind and hearing the voice of Jesus during an everyday journey, Saul immediately became Paul, the missionary who on countless occasions faced death because he refused to deny the reality of Christ's resurrection. As with the disciples, it's highly unlikely that he would have gone through such a radical transformation *and* risked his life if Jesus had not indeed risen from the dead.

"It can be asserted with confidence that men and women disbelieve the Easter story not because of the evidence but in spite of it."

—*J. N. D. Anderson, lawyer and institute director at the University of London*[9]

It's All in the Evidence

What evidence do we have for the resurrection of Christ beyond testimonies of the empty tomb, the numerous appearances of Jesus corroborated by several credible eyewitnesses, the instantaneous and absolute change in the disciples, and the complete silence of Jewish and Roman authorities (ever wonder why they were unable to silence the Christians?).

Well, there's proof found in the existence of the Church itself. In less than four centuries, Christianity became the Roman world's official religion. The entire religious social, legal and cultural systems of the Western world were altered because of Jesus. Despite centuries of rampant persecution, the Church has withstood the attacks and has continued to grow.

The Jewish system of worship—out of which Christianity sprang—was altered: The main day of worship changed from

Saturday—the Sabbath day the Jews had held sacred for thousands of years—to Sunday. This wasn't simply to test the faith
of football fans, but was directly related to celebrating and worshiping on the day of Jesus' resurrection.

Similarly, the doctrines of the Church quickly shifted to
embrace a Christological framework. If Christ hadn't risen, if
He was instead just another dead man, then why would the
Church preach of His deity from day one? In fact, believers
worldwide almost immediately embraced the risen Jesus as
the way, truth and life. The acceptance of His gospel message
became the determining factor for salvation.

Sunday Sources

The keeping of the Sabbath was such an important part of
Jewish culture that many theologians say that among the most
important arguments for the resurrection was the willingness
of the early Jewish Christians to celebrate the "Lord's Day," or
the first day of the week, instead of the Sabbath. It was a sign
that something defining, momentous, had happened.

Barnabas—yes, the same guy Saul/Paul visited after his
Damascus road experience—was a key figure in the Early Church.
His epistle, written in about A.D. 100, specifically mentions the
switch from the traditional Jewish Sabbath Saturday to Sunday,
the day of Jesus' resurrection: "Wherefore, also we keep the
eighth day with joyfulness, the day on which Jesus rose again
from the dead." But he wasn't the only one talking. Here is a brief
list of other authorities making reference to Christ's resurrection
and the Sunday worship by Christian believers:

- Pliny, a Roman governor in Asia Minor (A.D. 107), provides the earliest evidence of the Christian practice of
  celebrating Jesus' resurrection on Sunday in a letter in

which he wrote, "They were in the habit of meeting on a certain fixed day before it was light." Though the letter doesn't specifically mention Sunday (instead of the Jewish Sabbath of Saturday), most scholars who have examined the letter in full believe that the reference is clear.

- The epistle of Ignatius (in about A.D. 145-150), praised some who "were no longer observing the Sabbath." Ignatius was bishop of the church at Antioch, and his letter warned against those who required an observance of the Jewish law as a condition for salvation.

- Justin Martyr, writing in about A.D. 150, said this: "On the day called Sunday, all who live in cities or in the country gather together in one place, and the memoirs of the apostles or the writings of the prophets are read . . . Sunday is the day on which we all hold our common assembly, because it is the first day on which God, having wrought a change in the darkness and matter, made the world; and Jesus Christ our Saviour on the same day rose from the dead."

Others writing about this time indicate that by the end of the first century, and certainly by the end of the second century, the Sabbath was celebrated universally by the Christian Church. Among these writers are:

- Ireneaeus (A.D. 155-202)
- Dionysius, bishop in Greece (A.D. 170)
- Clement of Alexandria, Egypt (A.D. 194)
- Tertullian of Africa (A.D. 200)

Finally, there's the evidence found in the recorded writings of Early Church believers. Within the verses of the New Testament are portions that scholars call "creedal statements." Creeds were summarizations of Christian belief—basically statements of faith passed along orally. These were used, in the time before the New Testament was completed or copied, as an effective way to pass on known Christian truth. The relation of Early Christian creeds to this part of Scripture is significant, as New Testament historian Michael Licona explains:

> Scholars identify several instances in which oral traditions have been copied into the writings that comprise the New Testament . . . These are significant, since the oral tradition had to exist prior to the New Testament writings in order for the New Testament authors to include them. This takes us back to some of the earliest teachings of the Christian church, teachings that predate the writing of the New Testament.[10]

Through these early teachings and their New Testament preservation, we discover at least 40 creedal formulas that Early Christians knew about Jesus:

1. Jesus was really born in human flesh (see Phil. 2:6; 1 Tim. 3:16; 1 John 4:2)
2. Family line descended from David (see Acts 13:23; Rom. 1:3-4; 2 Tim. 2:8)
3. Implication of His baptism (see Rom. 10:9)
4. His word was preached (see 1 Tim. 3:16)
5. People believed in His message (see 1 Tim. 3:16)
6. Came from the town of Nazareth (see Acts 2:22; 4:10; 5:38)
7. John preceded Jesus' ministry (see Acts 10:37; 13:24-25)

8. Jesus' ministry began in Galilee (see Acts 10:37)

9. Jesus' ministry expanded to Judea (see Acts 10:37)

10. Jesus performed miracles (see Acts 2:22; 10:38)

11. Jesus fulfilled numerous Old Testament prophecies (see Acts 2:25-31; 3:21-25; 4:11; 10:43; 13:27-37)

12. Jesus attended a dinner (see 1 Cor. 11:23)

13. This was on the evening of His betrayal (see 1 Cor. 11:23)

14. He gave thanks before this meal (see 1 Cor. 11:23)

15. Jesus shared bread and beverage (see 1 Cor. 11:23)

16. Jesus explained that the bread and drink represented His impending substitutionary death for sin (see 1 Cor. 11:23)

17. Jesus stood before Pilate (see Acts 3:13;13:28)

18. Jesus affirmed His identity as King of the Jews (see 1 Tim. 6:13)

19. Jesus was killed (see Acts 3:13-15; 13:27-29)

20. Jesus died for humanity's sin (see 1 Pet. 3:18; Rom. 4:25; 1 Tim. 2:6)

21. This execution was carried out despite His righteous life (see 1 Pet. 3:18)

22. His crucifixion was specified as the mode of death (see Acts 2:23,36; 4:10; 5:30; 10:39)

23. His crucifixion was performed in the city of Jerusalem (see Acts 10:39; 13:27)

24. His crucifixion was carried out by wicked men (see Acts 2:23)

25. Jesus was buried (see Acts 13:29)

26. After His death, Jesus resurrected (see Acts 2:24,31-32; 3:15,26; 4:10; 5:30; 10:40; 13:30-37; 2 Tim. 2:8)

27. Jesus resurrected on the third day (see Acts 10:40)

28. The risen Jesus appeared to His followers (see Acts 13:31)

29. In His resurrected state, Jesus ate with His disciples (see Acts 10:40-41)

30. His disciples were eyewitnesses of these events (see Acts 2:32; 3:15; 5:32; 10:39,41; 13:31)

31. After rising from the grave, Jesus ascended into heaven and was glorified and exalted (see Acts 2:33; 3:21; 5:31; 1 Tim. 3:16; Phil. 2:6)

32. The risen Jesus instructed that salvation be preached in His name (see Acts 2:38-39; 3:19-23; 4:11-12; 5:32; 10:42-43; 13:26,38-41)

33. The resurrection and subsequent events showed God's approval of Jesus by validating His person and message (see Acts 2:22-24,36; 3:13-15; 10:42; 13:32-33; Rom. 1:3-4; 10:9-10)

34. Jesus is called "the Son of God" (Acts 13:33; Rom. 1:3-4)

35. Jesus is called "Lord" (Luke 24:34; Acts 2:36; 10:36; Rom. 1:4; 10:9; Phil. 2:11)

36. Jesus is called "Christ" or "Messiah" (Acts 2:36,38; 3:18,20; 4:10; 10:36; Rom. 1:4; Phil. 2:11; 2 Tim. 2:8)

37. Jesus is called "Savior" (Acts 5:31; 13:23)

38. Jesus is called "Prince" (Acts 5:31)

39. Jesus is called "the Holy and Righteous One" (Acts 2:27; 3:14; 13:35)

40. It is said that—regarding His essential nature—Jesus is God (see Phil. 2:6)[11]

Who Do You Say I Am?

We began this chapter addressing the common objection regarding Jesus that I hear in my travels around the nation: What makes Him so special in comparison to other religious figures? We've discussed the various options of what Jesus could in fact be: myth, man, mystic, misrepresentation or the actual Messiah. We've established that the key evidence establishing Christ's uniqueness lies in His resurrection. And we've debunked the various antiresurrection theories that, hopefully by now, sound essentially preposterous. So what now?

In his book *Mere Christianity*, C. S. Lewis lists the options available to us in drawing a conclusion about Jesus. The author points out that, based on what we know from history, Jesus' true identity is somewhat hard to ignore:

> I am trying here to prevent any one saying the really foolish thing that people often say about Him: "I'm ready to accept Jesus as a great moral teacher, but I don't accept His claim to be God." That is the one thing we must not say. A man who was merely a man and said the sort of things Jesus said would not be a great moral teacher. He would either be a lunatic—on the level of a man who says he is a poached egg—or else he would be the Devil of Hell. You must make your choice. Either this man was, and is, the Son of God: or else a madman or something worse. You can shut Him up for a fool, you can spit at Him and kill Him as a demon; or you can fall at His feet and call Him Lord and God. But let us not come with any patronizing nonsense about His being a great human teacher. He has not left that open to us. He did not intend to.[12]

Lewis goes on to restate the apparent options in what's become a well-known phrase: Either Jesus was a lunatic, a liar or He was truly Lord. Today, we can add a fourth option to this list: legend. Thanks to individuals such as philosopher Bertrand Russell—who once claimed that "historically, it is doubtful whether Christ ever existed at all, and if He did we don't know anything about Him"—Jesus is now often thrown in the same category as Paul Bunyan.[13] To make His life and teachings a little more palatable, a bit easier to swallow, we've construed that Christ was nothing more than a fictitious, legendary figure.

On a *Larry King Live* interview, Ellen Johnson, at the time president of the American Atheists organization, boldly declared, "The reality is, there is not one shred of secular evidence there ever was a Jesus Christ. Jesus Christ and Christianity is a modern religion."[14] Many others have added to Johnson's claims by labeling those who believe in the "fairy tale" of Jesus as lacking intelligence.

However, at this point in the chapter it should be obvious that statements like those of Ellen Johnson are obviously motivated by an open hostility to Christians and a flagrant disregard for a robust historical record.

Indeed, the glib assertion that Jesus was not a historical person and that He never lived is a relatively recent objection to Christianity. It also shows what some call "cultural imperialism," which means that the beliefs of our own place and time are the only beliefs that could possibly be true. In the ancient world, Christ's literal existence was never doubted—even by archenemies of the faith![15] Historian Will Durant has identified at least 19 ancient sources that refer to Jesus Christ as a real person, some of which are listed below:

- Thallus (historian, wrote in A.D. 52; references Christ's crucifixion)
- Cornelius Tacitus (called "greatest historian of Ancient Rome," lived around A.D. 64-116; confirms that Christ "suffered under Pontius Pilate, Procurator of Judea")
- Gaius Suetonius (Roman historian, wrote in approximately A.D. 120)

- Emperor Trajan (contemporary with Pliny)
- Emperor Hadrian (A.D. 117-138)
- Lucian of Samosata (Greek satirist, A.D. 170; refers to Christians' worship of "a man," a "crucified sage" who is "their lawgiver")
- Mara Bar-Serapion (first-century Syrian writer, wrote about A.D. 70; says the Jews "executed their wise King." Places Jesus on the same level as other ancient leaders and gods, but says "the wise King" died for a good cause and His teachings live on in His followers)
- Phlegon (born A.D. 80; about A.D. 140 writes in reference to Jesus' suffering and the darkness that occurred at the time of His death)
- Plinius Secundus (also called "Pliny the Younger"; in A.D. 112 writes about the Christians' belief that Jesus was deity)
- Julianus Africanus (about A.D. 221; references Christ's death at Passover and the darkness that ensued)[16]

"Several Jewish writings also tell of His flesh-and-blood existence," writes author Larry Chapman. "Both Gemaras [the early rabbinic commentary] of the Jewish Talmud refer to Jesus. Although these consist of only a few, brief bitter passages intended to discount Jesus' Deity, these very early Jewish writings don't begin to hint that He was not a historical person."[17]

We also have the famous writings of Flavius Josephus, the son of Jewish religious leader Matthius. Josephus was born in A.D. 37, only a few years after Jesus died, and because of where and when he lived, he would have been familiar with facts about Jesus' life and teachings. Around A.D. 67, Josephus began writing as court historian for Roman emporer Vespasian, and almost 30 years later, in *Antiquities of the Jews*, he comments about Jesus as an actual person: "At that time lived Jesus, a holy man, if He may be called, for He performed wonderful works, and taught men, and joyfully received the truth. And He was followed by many Jews and Greeks. He was the Messiah." Josephus further authenticated that Jesus was tried by Pilate, accused by powerful Jewish leaders, was crucified and was seen alive three days later—"restored to life."[18]

Because the writings of Josephus come from so close to the time of Jesus' life, and because they so clearly identify specifics of His life and ministry, and because of modern archeological and linguistic scholarship, the text of Josephus has been in dispute. Did Josephus really write, "He was the Messiah"? Or did he write, as some say, "He was believed to be the Messiah"?

These are certainly important questions, but whatever future scholarship brings, it will not overturn the key points I want to make here: From the very first century, there are authentic historical accounts of a real Jesus. To assert otherwise, as Ellen Johnson and others do, is to ignore a great weight of evidence and to replace it with wishful thinking.

In Favor of Jesus

Did you hear about the two men arguing over the life of Jesus who decided to settle their disagreement in court? (Sounds like the start of a bad joke, doesn't it?) The two Italians, both in their 70s, had grown up together in the same village and had known each other their entire lives. But they'd gotten into a verbal sparring match over religion. One man had become a priest; the other had become a skeptic. (I know, I know . . . it *still* sounds like a joke!)

Because the skeptic harbored angry feelings toward the Church and Christians, he eventually turned against his lifelong friend. Among other things, the guy accused the priest of "tricking the people" in teaching them about Jesus. As of the time of this writing, the men were set to go before a judge and argue over whether Jesus really lived or not. The judge would then rule based on who presented the best evidence.[19]

While such a story may sell newspapers today, the records of history solidified the facts about Jesus long ago. Respected historian Edwin Yamauchi states, "From time to time some people have tried to deny the existence of Jesus, but this really is a lost cause. There is overwhelming evidence that Jesus did exist, and these hypothetical questions are really very vacuous and fallacious." Yamauchi, who was raised Buddhist but who later became a Christian, adds, "The fact is that we have better historical documentation for Jesus than for the founder of any other ancient religion."[20]

Cambridge University professor Dr. Michael Grant goes so far as to say, "In recent years, no serious scholar has ventured to postulate the non-history of Jesus."[21] The key word there is "serious." It's easy to accept the beliefs of whoever talks the loudest or appears the most on CNN. Unfortunately, our culture has bought into the deceptive theories intended to refute Jesus as Lord. Millions of people casually dismiss Jesus as just a fairy-tale character or even as never having existed simply because that's the popular, convenient thing to believe. Yet the closer we examine these arguments, the more we realize that this is yet another case of the public heaping praise on a naked Emperor parading through town.

"Jesus was a historical not a mythical being. No remote or foul myth obtruded itself on the Christian believer; his faith was founded on positive, historical and acceptable facts."
—*Clifford Herschel Moore, Harvard University professor*[22]

Jesus is for real—that fact is historically verifiable. But He's not just another great man in history. Don't insult Him by clumping Him in with the Napoleons and Einsteins. The Bible claims that Jesus is "the way and the truth and the life" (John 14:6, *NIV*). Its various accounts testify that He is the true Son of God, sent by the Father to redeem and reconcile all humanity. And with proof—solid evidence—we can know that that is indeed the truth.

Summary Response

Reasons to acknowledge Jesus' uniqueness:

Because of His identity
Because of His message
Because of His credentials
Because of the facts

Jesus Is Not the Only Way to Heaven

Common Objection:
"Aren't there many roads to heaven?
Don't all paths lead to the same place?"

Christians disagree about a lot of things. As I travel the country to speak on college campuses, I often get questions from Christians about evolution, worship styles or whether speaking in tongues is the real deal or not.

But most atheists, agnostics and skeptics look at these intra-Christian agreements either not at all or with some humor. "Who cares?" they often say. The real problem *they* have with Christianity is one that most Christians—at least Christians throughout history—actually take for granted. It's a question that is at the core of the value system of a postmodern, relativistic world: the issue of Christianity's exclusivity.

If there's one thing that Americans don't want to hear, it's that their neighbor Joe, a super-nice guy who serves at a soup kitchen every holiday and who dabbles in Buddhism every once in a while, might be going to hell. We don't like to offend people, especially when it comes to matters of faith. We'd rather give everyone a gold star for effort and celebrate our spiritual diversity. In short, we like inclusivity.

Can't We All Just Get Along?

It's not hard to see how we got here. When you take God out of the equation of life (as evolution has done), it affects your absolutes. When you take God's Word out of the public places (as the 1963 Supreme Court decision *Murray v. Curlett*—and others—did by taking prayer and the Bible out of the public schools), it affects your absolutes. And although it may sound paradoxical, when you take God's merciful judgment out of salvation (a practice I and many others call "spiritual relativism"), it affects your absolutes.

When people cease to believe in absolutes, foundational biblical truths appear to be incoherent. So it is no wonder that some of the most important teachings of Scripture are now almost completely misunderstood or rejected. For example, almost 80 percent of all people believe there's more than one way to get to heaven. *Ninety-one percent* of Catholics agree with this view. Maybe the most telling, however, is this statistic: 68 percent of evangelical Protestants say a good person who is of a different religious faith will still go to heaven.[1] And 65 percent of evangelical teens say you can't be sure which religion is right.[2]

Don't try blaming atheism. That's not the problem today. Survey after survey proves that we are a deeply "spiritual" people. No, the problem today is that people have bought into the wrong spirit. Classic writer G. K. Chesterton states it this way: "When people cease to believe in God, they do not believe in nothing, they believe in anything." And that is the danger we face today in our hyper-spiritualized world that's forgotten Jehovah and turned to an iPod version of God—choose your own mix.

"Organized interest in atheism has lagged because the opposition isn't as strong as it used to be. There has been considerable liberalizing of religion and the lines of conflict aren't nearly as strong."

—Joseph Preston of the Free Thinkers of America[3]

Feelings, Nothing More Than Feelings

In a telling article on the diversified, inclusive state of spirituality in America today, *Newsweek* writer Jerry Adler aptly stated, "Today . . . the real spiritual quest is not to put another conservative on the Supreme Court, or to get creation science into the schools. If you experience God directly, your faith is not going to hinge on whether natural selection could have produced the flagellum of a bacterium. If you feel God within you, then the important question is settled; the rest is details."[4]

"If you *feel* God within you . . ." After all, that's what it's all about, right? Tragically, feelings have become this culture's barometer of truth. The "if it feels good" mantra has become so ingrained in us that it's beyond cliché. Our diet, fitness, career and relationship choices have become all about feeling good about ourselves; why should God be any different? As a result, God—in whatever form you chose Him—is seen merely as a "life coach" to get you from point A to a much-better-you point B. "Rather than being about a god who commands you, it's about finding a religion that empowers you," comments Alan Wolfe, director of the Boisi Center for Religion and American Public Life at Boston College, on the individualism stressed in "Americanized" faith.[5]

"Truth, morality and meaning are connected. If the first goes, everything else goes with it. Jesus established not merely the existence of truth but His own pristine embodiment of truth. To reject Him is to choose to govern oneself with a lie."

—Ravi Zacharias, apologist[6]

Not That There's Anything Wrong with That

"So what's the problem?" some may counter. "If a personalized, subjective view of God makes you become a better person, what's to fault?"

There are many problems with trusting our feelings alone to define our spiritual health—the nature of God and our relationship with Him. To understand that, consider how a person might feel when he has a life-threatening disease, such as cancer. Often, people do not even know they have cancer until a routine physical examination reveals it. Many people who are diagnosed with cancer for the first time have this reaction: "How can that be? I feel great."

Then, of course, the treatment begins. To aggressively fight a tough disease such as cancer requires strong medicine—medicine that can make the patient feel perfectly miserable. But it is important to remember that although the patient feels worse, he is actually getting better.

Finally, there are also the ongoing ups and downs of life. Ask a cancer survivor after he has come through the process and been declared cancer free how he feels about life, and often he will say something about a new perspective. "The little ups and downs of life don't bother me as much," he might say. "I don't let circumstances affect my attitude."

I say all of that to make this point: Feelings are important. God gave them to us for many good reasons. But they are, by themselves, poor guides in life. By themselves, they often lead us away from, not toward, reality and the truth. In some ways, feelings are like the needle on a compass. They make for a great guide so long as there is a fixed magnetic North Pole in your world. But if your world has no fixed North Pole, or if you allow other forces to spin your needle, it becomes worthless and deceptive as a guide.

So our own experience tells us, when we're being honest with ourselves, that feelings should not be our ultimate guide. And—more to the point here—God said so, too.

Ah, the dreaded "God said" phrase. It's a modern-day religion major's nightmare. How can one person's God say it's okay to indulge in hedonistic pleasures (as long as you ask for forgiveness in the end), while another's encourages killing any unbelievers? What gives?

Maybe a little recapping of what we've already established in this book will help. So far, we've recognized three essential truths to this case: God is real; the Bible, as His Word, is verifiably authentic, accurate and trustworthy; and Jesus Christ lived, died and fulfilled His claim of being God's Son by being resurrected. If we agree that the Bible is indeed God's Word and that Jesus is the Son of God, then both of these sources are the ultimate truth. And it was Jesus, as that ultimate truth, who said, "I am the way, the truth, and the life. No one comes to the Father except through Me" (John 14:6).

He followed up His "gotta come through Me" message with other bold statements:

- "All things have been delivered to Me by My Father, and no one knows the Son except the Father. Nor does anyone know the Father except the Son, and the one to whom the Son wills to reveal Him" (Matt. 11:27).

- "For this cause I was born, and for this cause I have come into the world, that I should bear witness to the truth. Everyone who is of the truth hears My voice" (John 18:37).

- "For my Father's will is that everyone who looks to the Son and believes in Him shall have eternal life, and I will raise him up at the last day" (John 6:40, *NIV*).

- "I tell you the truth, he who believes has everlasting life" (John 6:47, *NIV*).

- "And as Moses lifted up the serpent in the wilderness, even so must the Son of Man be lifted up, that whoever believes in Him should not perish but have eternal life. For God so loved the world that He gave His only begotten Son, that whoever believes in Him should not perish but have everlasting life. For God did not send His Son into the world to condemn the world, but that the world through Him might be saved" (John 3:14-17).

- "I give [My followers] eternal life, and they shall never perish; no one can snatch them out of My hand. My Father, who has given them to Me, is greater than all; no one can snatch them out of My Father's hand. I and the Father are one" (John 10:28-30, *NIV*).

- "I am the resurrection and the life. He who believes in me will live, even though he dies; and whoever lives and believes in Me will never die" (John 11:25-26, *NIV*).

- "If you abide in My word, you are My disciples indeed. And you shall know the truth, and the truth shall make you free" (John 8:31-32).

- "Therefore whoever confesses Me before men, him I will also confess before My Father who is in heaven. But whoever denies Me before men, him I will also deny before My Father who is in heaven" (Matt. 10:32-33).

Talk about being *exclusive*!

Bragging Rights

Remember life on the school playground as a youngster? There was always that new kid who would come in and cause a near fight on the grounds because, according to him, his dad was the greatest man who ever lived (and, it followed, could beat up your dad). At that age, of course, that meant his father was a fireman, a police officer, a racecar driver or, in the *extremely* rare but cool case, an astronaut.

For the rest of the day, rumors would swirl. "So-and-so's dad is an astronaut!" Of course you, being exponentially superior to your naive peers, wouldn't believe it until you saw it for yourself. And so sometime later you'd bicycle over to the new kid's house and hang around in the bushes past your dinner-time waiting for this near-mythological figure to come home. And, as fate would have it, nine times out of ten the newbie would be right. All it took for you to believe in the boy's claims was one look at Dad.

As we have already seen in previous chapters, Jesus has given us ample evidence regarding the truth of His claims about both Himself and God—the most dramatic evidence being the resurrection itself.

So when Jesus claims that He is the only way to salvation, the sole gatekeeper of heaven, we must evaluate it in light of everything else we now know about Him. And when we do that, we see that to reject this claim actually requires much more faith and much less reliance on logic, history and experience than simply accepting Jesus at His word.

Jesus wasn't just pulling His material out of thin air. His life demonstrated that. His resurrection confirmed who He was and what He taught. By His coming back to life, He proved beyond a shadow of a doubt that He was indeed the Son of God and that He therefore had every right to not only "boast" in His Dad, but also to claim Himself as the only way to eternal life.

"And many will follow their destructive ways, because of whom the way of truth will be blasphemed" (2 Pet. 2:2).

An Unpopular Club Membership

Political correctness and the mind-set of the day both say that all religious viewpoints are equally true at the same time. Beneath the surface is the assumption that they all say the same things: follow the Golden Rule, be a good person, give to the needy, and so forth. But all propositions—because some will inevitably be in contradiction—obviously can't be true at the same time. And as you can see from the following chart, the world's religions, despite any apparent similarities, are at their core contradictory to Christianity.

The Words That Count

Of the issues listed on this chart, none seem to captivate people more than the prospect of heaven. The notion of an afterlife has fascinated us for centuries. In December 2005, ABC News correspondent Barbara Walters hosted the TV special "Heaven: Where Is It? How Do We Get There?" and interviewed leaders of various faiths on their views of heaven. Her lineup included such notables as the Dalai Lama and atheist Ellen Johnson, who matter-of-factly declared:

> Heaven doesn't exist, hell doesn't exist. We weren't alive before we were born and we're not going to exist after we die. I'm not happy about the fact that that's the end of life, but I can accept that and make my life more fulfilling now, because this is the only chance I have.[7]

In the midst of other "all-inclusive" faiths, Christianity stuck out like a sore thumb. And yet that's exactly how Jesus defined it. Christ was explicit in answering the claim that all roads lead to heaven: *"No one comes to the Father except through Me."* Yes, that includes Buddhists, Muslims, Hindus and anyone else worshiping another god. But it also includes the "good ol' boy" who assumes he's going to heaven because he's always tried to do the right thing. It includes the couple that has been in church every time the doors are open but who have never accepted Jesus as their savior. And it includes you and me—if we do not profess that Jesus is Lord and seek *His* salvation.

The key is this: We did not define the terms of entering the kingdom of heaven. God did. And if we acknowledge Him and allow Him the inherent rights as God, then we can suppose that His words carry more weight than ours. So when Jesus—God in flesh—says He is the *only* way, then that's the truth. No piecemeal version of salvation. No cut-and-paste God who grants the rewards of heaven on our terms. Jesus, by His rightful account, is indeed the *only* way.

Is it any wonder our culture scoffs at such an absolute?

Belief Systems

	Christianity	Judaism	Islam	Mormonism	Jehovah's Witnesses
Primary Founder: ➡	Jesus Christ	Abraham	Mohammed	Joseph Smith	Charles Russell

Teachings on:

	Christianity	Judaism	Islam	Mormonism	Jehovah's Witnesses
God	One, eternal, Triune, righteous, wise, loving, merciful	One, eternal, just	Allah, one, eternal	Once a man, who later became a god	Jehovah, but not at all like the God of the Bible
Man	Sinful, but valuable to God	Basically good with "flaws," learns through suffering	Basically good	People will become gods who will be worshipped	Basically good, spiritual needs can be earned
Scripture	The Bible (inspired and infallible)	The Torah (the Old Testament)	The Koran	Book of Mormon and Pearl of Great Price	Jehovah Witnesses' version of the Bible *only* and certain other publications
Jesus Christ	Fully God, fully man, deity	Ignored, distorted or "respectfully rejected."	A prophet, a man, not the Son of God	An "elder brother" who became a god	Just a man, denied, distorted
Life's purpose	To know God through a relationship with Jesus Christ	To love God (Deut. 6:5), and to try to do good	To submit to Allah	To be a part of the "one true Church" (the LDS church)	To win others to the Jehovah Witnesses faith and thereby earn heaven
Heaven	Place of eternal joy for those who have received God's gift of salvation in Jesus	If there is one, we'll all be there	For those chosen by Allah	Planet Kolob; celestial kingdom; terrestrial kingdom; telestial kingdom	For 144,000 faithful Jehovah Witnesses
Hell	Place of eternal torment for those who have rejected God's love	For evil people	For those rejected by Allah	No real hell, just lower levels of heaven	For non-Jehovah's Witnesses

Belief Systems

	Hinduism	Bhuddism	New Age/misc. "spirituality"	Secularism
Primary Founder: ➡	no one founder	Siddhartha Gautama	1960s culture	various humanists

Teachings on:

	Hinduism	Bhuddism	New Age/misc. "spirituality"	Secularism
God	Thirty-three main gods	No God, only "divine consciousness"	Pantheism (God is the universe)	Doesn't exist
Man	Part of god (Brahman, the main god)	Good, part of god, though god doesn't really exist	Good, even divine, part of God	The ultimate authority for all things
Scripture	The Vedas	Four noble truths and the eight-fold path	No one authoritative book	None
Jesus Christ	Ignored or distorted	An avatar, shaman, mystic	Didn't exist, or if he did was only a man	Just a man
Life's purpose	To work out bad karma through knowledge, devotion or good deeds	There is no real "truth," but you *should* empty yourself	To gain power, self-realization, godhood	None, or if there is a purpose, it is to usher in utopia
Heaven	Nirvana, where you are *mukti:* free from all desires	Emptiness, the end of consciousness, thought ceases	None; in the mind; here on Earth	There isn't one, or maybe we can turn Earth into "heaven"
Hell	Here on Earth, being trapped in reincarnations	No such thing as sin, so no need for punishment	None; or ignorance; or for evil people	No such thing

Summary Response

Reasons to reject the belief that "all roads lead to heaven":

Logical view that opposite roads lead to different destinations
Impossibility that contradictory assertions can all be true
Unmistakable clarity of the Bible's teaching
Legitimate authority that Jesus has to speak on the subject
Irrelevance of popular opinion to the contrary

A Loving God Wouldn't Send People to Hell

Common Objection:
"Is hell for real? If so, how can a loving God send people there?"

We're all familiar with this cartoonish picture: a mean-looking red guy with horns on his head, a pitchfork in his hand and a black cape draping down to his goat-like lower half. It's the devil, of course, standing in a cave amid the stalagmites, stalactites and fiery flames. (If you go by *The Far Side* artist Gary Larson's depiction, he's adjusting the thermostat from "hot" to "hotter" to "hot as hell.") With a single motion, Satan summons his minions to crack their whips on the backs of the marching slaves bound by chains. And every now and then, we hear the echoing screams of those in agony.

Just as humans have wrestled with the concept of heaven for thousands of years, so also hell has received the same treatment. Artists have tried to imagine its surroundings. Musicians have sung of its terrors (though some treat it as a vacation home). But through it all, it has remained otherworldly. Plastic. Dreamlike. Even comical to some. And, ultimately, unreal to most.

Why else would its name be tossed around so flippantly? Why would friends jokingly tell each other to go there? How else can we explain the way it is handled as a meaningless, harmless

concoction of religious fanatics? In fact, many feel that the concept of hell—and indeed it's treated as such—merely arose during a time when people were primitive and simply didn't know
any better. Like a ghost story being shared around a campfire to
rouse a good scare, tales of a horrific underworld were supposedly made up by simpletons trying to personify evil. And so hell is
nothing more than a farcical tale—sometimes spooky, sometimes
eerie, but never real. Fast forward a couple hundred years, and it's
still handled the same—only now our ghost story inventions are
projected on a big screen and earn millions at the box office.

Life Isn't a Movie

For those a little more inclined to the "supernatural," hell is a
spiritual realm that exists here on Earth. The best this world
has to offer is considered "heavenly," while the worst things are
"hellish." Still others say they'd rather be in hell since (they
assume) "that's where the crowd I run with will probably be!"
Better to live it up as you go down in flames than maintain a
boring life of constant goodness on your way to heaven.

It's this very mind-set that has made hell "cool," while heaven
is treated as nothing more than an eternal bore. Even Christians
who recognize hell as a dreadful place fall into the trap of
thinking that heaven will surely be dull—an eternity of singing
"Kumbaya" refrains in monotonous tranquility. As a result, our
brash culture continues its fixation on hedonism in the name of
enjoying every flesh-filled moment to its fullest.

The truth is, life—and the afterlife—would not be treated so
lightly were there a true revelation of its gravity. Hell is no figment
of the imagination. The Bible—which we've already established as
truth handed to us by God Himself—lays out the facts. And the
biblical account conflicts significantly with many of these popular notions. From the biblical account, we learn this about hell:

1. The *location* of hell is reached only by death.
2. The *conditions* of hell are eternal suffering.
3. The *occupants* of hell are there due to sin.

An in-depth study of hell is well beyond the scope of my intentions here. If we did that study, we would discover that there are accounts of hell in both the Old Testament and the New Testament. We would learn that Jesus described it as a place "where the fire never goes out" (Mark 9:43, *NIV*). He repeatedly depicts hell as "outside" the kingdom of God, a place of darkness where "there will be weeping and gnashing of teeth" (Matt. 25:30).

"Historically, hell has been portrayed in evangelical sermons as fire and brimstone. The most we should say is that hell is a place of unexplainable mystery. The reality is probably far worse than our most vivid imaginations can conjure up. The reality of both heaven and hell are both greater than we can express . . . While it's very important to teach and preach about the reality of hell, it should be done only with evangelical tears. There is sometimes a kind of gloating that people are broiling in hell. I don't think that honors God or reflects the love of Jesus. We should shed tears over those who are perishing."

—Timothy George, author and dean of the Beeson Divinity School at Samford University[1]

There is much that we do not yet know about either heaven or hell. For example, Scripture uses the words "Hades" and "Sheol" to describe a place or condition where the departed dead who are unsaved await God's final judgment. Some of these distinctions are hotly debated by biblical scholars.

But if either Jesus or Scripture itself are credible in any way—and if you've read this far, you know that I've offered tremendous evidence of the trustworthiness of both—then there is one thing we can say for sure: Heaven and hell are real. As Jonathan Edwards said about hell, "'Tis dreadful, 'tis awful . . . but 'tis true."

Maybe If I Pretend It's Not Real . . .

This is the story of two Christian young men serving in the military. For several weeks on the field, the two soldiers had listened to their unit chaplain explain away many parts of the Bible, which was disturbing to them. The chaplain's modern twists on theology were beginning to affect many of the soldiers who formerly had a robust faith. Finally, the two soldiers went privately to talk with the chaplain about his less-than-biblical theology. Eventually in the conversation, the subject of hell came up.

"Today scholars know that hell isn't exactly what people thought it was for many centuries," the chaplain began. "God is *love*. Eternal punishment and hell have, for centuries, been spoken of in too literal a sense."

"So you're saying that you don't believe in hell?" one soldier asked.

"No, I don't," responded the chaplain.

The soldiers began to walk away from his tent. "See you both at the services Sunday?" the chaplain called out.

"I doubt it," one of the men said.

The chaplain look surprised. "Why not?"

With childlike faith and consistent logic, one soldier answered, "Think about it, chaplain. If there's no hell, we don't need you. And if there is a hell, we don't want to be misled."

Hell is for real, despite today's softening of the truth. It isn't a matter of being scared out of your wits. Neither is it just the antiheaven locale. Hell, at its core, is the worst possible place in existence: a place eternally apart from God. Regardless of how terrifying our modern-day horror-movie depictions of hell can get, they pale in comparison to the actual torment that arises out of being forever in need of God yet forever separate from Him.

The Ultimate Reconciliation

Earlier, I said that there is much about hell that is mysterious, much about it that we don't fully know. However, Scripture is not at all silent on the issue, and later in this chapter we will identify 11 things we can know about hell from the biblical account.

In my travels around the country, speaking to both believers and nonbelievers alike about the evidence for Christianity, I find that the main question people have about hell is this: "How could a loving God send people to hell?" So before we dig too deeply into what the Bible says about hell, let's tackle this important question.

First, those of us who believe the biblical accounts know that God is love (see 1 John 4:8). Although it's one of the countless core aspects of who He is, for those who have been saved by His love, it's undoubtedly His most precious trait. What's interesting to me is that even many skeptics and unbelievers harbor a hope that this is true. In fact, the question about hell—"How could a loving God send people to hell?"—has implicit in it the assumption that God is a loving God.

Yet among those wonderful attributes is another essential one that must not be forgotten: God is just (see Deut. 32:4). Justice is as important an attribute of God's character as love. The two are not mutually exclusive, nor do they conflict in any way. Earlier, you may remember, we introduced the notion that some ideas are paradoxical. A paradox is a set of statements that appear to contradict themselves but are in fact both true. We humans, especially in our modern age, during a time when basic logic is often not taught in our schools, often get tripped up on this idea, because in our finite minds we can barely, if ever, comprehend a perfect blend of the two.

Thankfully, God is not obligated to change who He is because of what we may wrongly assume or because of the limits of our ability to grasp His limitlessness. (If He were, we'd have an inconsistent God who changes His nature with the wind.) We, on the other hand, are obligated to amend our lives in light of what God has plainly disclosed. And His message to the world is this: I, in My righteousness, cannot tolerate sin.

Obviously, that's not good news to us. We're sinful. (Don't believe that? Check out the next chapter.) Our state of being, which is by nature against God, puts us directly in line of God's righteous, holy indignation against sin. And what are the consequences of sin? Death (see Rom. 6:23). Hell. Eternal separation from God. When He formed existence, God established a place for sin and rebellion against Him: hell. Does He desire any of His own creation to go there? Not on your life.

Just as we know from Scripture that heaven and hell are real, we know that God is good, righteous, gracious and merciful. The entire gospel story—Jesus coming to Earth to be sacrificed in our place—is couched in His lovingkindness and mercy toward us. He offers us forgiveness and redemption for our natural condition of opposition to Him. Even then, in His unmerited love, He does not force that forgiveness on us. It must be accepted. At His core, this loving God shudders at the notion of His beloved—you, me . . . all people—spending eternity away from Him.

In fact, an interesting side note is the amount of attention hell is given in God's Word in comparison to how much time is spent discussing heaven. While heaven is mentioned or alluded to hundreds of times in Scripture, hell is only referred to 32 times in the *New King James Version* (only 14 times in the *New International Version*). God is more concerned about painting us a picture of what *should* be than what *might* be. He's not counting on a worst-case scenario!

I could easily see, however, how some people could understand and accept that God is love, and that it is necessary to accept Jesus as Savior, and still say, "But come on, does God still have to send people to hell to suffer forever?" Why not just some sort of punishment that lasts for a while? Or why not just some sort of annihilation of their souls so that they don't get to be in heaven but they don't have to suffer hell either?

This last idea is one that is common in some circles. It is called "annihilationism." Seventh-Day Adventists and even some evangelicals believe that if someone dies apart from Christ, they are simply unconscious, or have their soul annihilated, for all eternity.

There are two problems with this idea. The first problem is that it is not supported by any shred of Scripture. In short, it is not a biblical teaching.

But the second problem should be obvious even to those who do not accept Scripture as the true guide to belief. Allow me to share with you a rather outlandish scenario that, while ridiculous, makes the point I am trying to get you to see. Imagine that you are standing at the edge of a huge pool of toxic fluid, but you don't know that it's toxic. It looks like a swimming pool to you, and you're thinking about jumping in. If I come along and say, "Don't jump in that pool. Come over here and jump in my pool instead. You'll have a much better time. It's much cleaner. Over here it's all good," you may or may not find that argument convincing. You might say, "I understand, but this pool is right here, and it looks okay to me. I think I'll just jump in right here."

Of course, if I cared anything at all about you, I would tell you the rest of the story. I would say, "No. Don't do that. It is a toxic pool, filled with acid. You will surely die."

So it is with hell. God does not want us to go to hell. But evil's existence makes hell a reality. To pretend that it is not a reality is perhaps the least loving, the least merciful thing either God or His followers could possibly do if we want to lead people into the loving embrace of Christ.

What Do You Know?

So while the arguments above do not irrefutably prove the existence of hell, they do point us to 11 important facts regarding the subject of hell.

1. The Bible (our authority on matters of eternity) clearly affirms the reality of hell (see Rev. 20:11-15).

2. Jesus Christ taught and affirmed the reality of hell (see Matt. 25:31-46).

3. Humans are morally accountable to God. Since the Garden of Eden, God gave us volitional faculties that we exercise on a daily basis. For those who ultimately acknowledge His Son, Jesus, as Lord, God has a place prepared in heaven. But He has also provided a place in eternity for those who choose to reject Him. This ultimate destination is called hell.

4. To deny the reality of hell undermines the fixed nature of Christian revelation. In previous chapters, we established that every word in the Bible was given by divine revelation: The Holy Spirit moved upon writers. In the book that would close the canon of Scripture, the Holy Spirit, moving upon John, issued a warning to anyone who would tamper with the

book of Revelation or with His written revelation: "For I testify to everyone who hears the words of the prophecy of this book: If anyone adds to these things, God will add to him the plagues that are written in this book; and if anyone takes away from the words of the book of this prophecy, God shall take away his part from the Book of Life, from the holy city, and from the things which are written in this book" (22:18-19).

So what does this have to do with the reality of hell? It's safe to say that every biblical passage about hell is true. And since we know the biblical doctrine of hell *was* true, then it must *still* be true. God's Word is not intermittently accurate.

Your car's windshield wipers might have the nifty feature of intermittence. They stop . . . then they go. They're off . . . then they're on. That may be okay for car wipers, but the nature of Scripture is in no way intermittent. If the Bible was entirely true, then it currently remains entirely true. And tomorrow it will *still* be entirely true.

If hell was somehow true but no longer is, then the Bible's accuracy is somehow sporadic. Since the content of the Bible contains both affirmations of hell and prohibitions against biblical revisionism, then it is only logical that the doctrine of hell remains in the teachings of the Church.

5. The reality of hell is intricately tied to the *person* and *work* of Christ. If there is no hell, then our understanding of who Jesus Christ is and what He did must be thoroughly revised. However, He clearly sets the record straight in Revelation 1:18, showing His conquering work of hell that was accomplished on the cross: "I am He who lives, and was dead, and

behold, I am alive forevermore. Amen. And I have the keys of Hades and of Death."

6. The reality of hell does not compromise God's love. Let's pause for a second and examine the second part of this chapter's question: *How could a loving God send people to hell?*

Yet the truth still remains: hell exists. And that leads us to the next group of sobering facts . . .

7. Hell is necessary because God's just nature demands that wickedness be punished. Since we all fall short of God's standard of righteousness (see Rom. 3:10), we all deserve hell. It is completely fair that some go to hell. Actually, *any* of us going to heaven is what is completely *unfair*. How so? Because the same law God established to separate Himself from wickedness condemns us to that very separation. The divine, established laws of this universe don't let a sinner off the hook. Sin has consequences—eternal consequences. While we're on Earth, we see glimpses of sin's ramifications, yet at the end of all life is when the utmost consequence of heaven or hell is faced.

This idea is hard for us humans to take because we do not have the kind of revulsion from sin, evil and wickedness that God has—or that we indeed should have. Even the best of us flirt with sin. We smile and wink at it. We too often forget that one single sin equates to death. That's one reason why when we encounter God's perfectly just and appropriate response to the sin He sees in our lives, we want to call His reaction "unfair"— because in those moments of encounter with God's holiness and justice, we also see most clearly our sinfulness, and our entire being recoils from those encounters (see Isa. 59:2). As humans, most of us know in our hearts, when we're being honest with ourselves, that we all automatically qualify for death row. This isn't just a club for murderers, extortionists, rapists . . . those who've done the *really big* bad things. Nope; a single time of going against God makes you eligible for hell (see Jas. 2:10; Rom. 3:23).

What is unfair, then, is that God would provide a way for us to escape His just wrath (again, not against us but against our sinfulness). Somehow, in the midst of this bleakest of situations, Jesus made a way. As the lone perfect being, He came to save the day. The only person who could fulfill the law stepped out of heaven, willed Himself through persecution, death and unimaginable torment, and satisfied the requirements of sin—*for all time*! He didn't have to humble Himself to the point of being "despised and rejected by men" (Isa. 53:3), yet He did for our sake . . . just so that we could be with Him in heaven (see John 14:6; 1 Pet. 3:18; Phil. 2:8; Col. 2:13-15).

8. Hell is necessary because man is not really seeking God but is actually running away from Him. How can I say this with confidence? Once again, it comes down to our natural state of sin. Left to our own devices, we wouldn't choose to follow God—we'd choose to go our own way. Maybe not at first . . . but eventually.

Still, God allows people to have their preference. I can't tell you the number of times people have asked me why God didn't just create us "right" in the first place. If His original desire is for us to live with Him in His glorious perfection, why didn't He just make us sinless? The answer falls upon one simple yet profound word: love.

Love—that core element of who God is—stirred our Maker to create us in His image, with the same capacity to experience love.

Basically, we were created to experience Him. Yet being molded in His image also means we are free, like Him, to withhold or express that love. And that results in a freedom of choice. Love, by its very nature, makes us incapable of being robots. Our capacity to love also gives us a capacity to reject Him.

Consider the following syllogism formed by French philosopher and mathematician Blaine Pascal: "All who seek God will find Him. Not all find God. Therefore (despite appearances), not all really sought God."[2] It's sad but true. In fact, it's terrifying when we consider the ramifications of knowing this love—knowing God—and yet opting to shun it.

9. In the Day of Judgment, the condemned will not be so because they haven't heard of Jesus; the condemned will be consigned to hell because they violated the clear moral standard that they really did know yet chose to reject (see Rom. 2:12-16).

10. Final ordering, reckoning and closure seem not only proper but to be desired. If there is no "final reckoning," no culmination to history and no final reward, then it seems to me that many of the longings of the human heart will go unrequited. God made us to desire closure, finality, *resolution*. We see it throughout art—stories, dramas, even music theorists say that the final chord of a piece of music *resolves*. How satisfying would it be (and how appropriate would it be) if God never fully restored order to the universe He created? Not very satisfying. How excited would we be if there was no end in sight to God being mocked and ignored on Earth? Not excited. Sadly, satisfaction and excitement over these things display the other side of the coin . . .

11. Rejecting God's infinite love merits deserved eternal punishment. In other words, there is serious guilt in choosing *self* and *sin* over *Redeemer* and *rescue*. We were born to be with God. Yet doing so, because of our natural state, requires being saved. And if we know of a Savior yet decide to try and save ourselves, we alone must face the consequences of our inadequacy (see John 1:12).

C. S. Lewis poignantly said, "Some will not be redeemed. There is no doctrine which I would more willingly remove from Christianity than this, if it lay in my power. But it has the full support of Scripture, and specially, of our Lord's own words; it has always been held by Christendom; and it has the support of reason. If a game is played, it must be possible to lose it."[3]

But Surely Not . . .

Earlier, we spent some time talking about people who rejected Christ. We said that hell provided a powerful motivation for them to accept the saving love of Jesus. That was a partial answer to the question: "How could a loving God send people to hell?"

But there is another part to that question that I get all the time. It's what I call the Africa question: "Yeah, but what about all the people in Africa, Asia or any remote place who never hear about Jesus? How could God send them to hell?"

Allow me to share a couple of personal examples to shed some light on this. A few years ago, I met a man from Papua New Guinea. He grew up as an aborigine, having never heard the name of God or Jesus Christ. Yet even as a young boy, he would look to the sky and pray, "God, I want to know You." Was he specifically praying to Jehovah? Did he know anything about the gospel story? Of course not. But he was aware of his need, so much so that he would try to appease the gods—any god—by cutting himself. His tribe believed that there were spirits alive in the woods. So in an act of sacrifice, he would viciously gouge his arms, thinking the more pain he brought on himself, the more pleased these gods that haunted him would be.

"Even as I did that, I knew it wasn't right," he told me. "I wanted to know the true God. I knew there had to be a real God beyond the gods in the trees." Years later he heard of some Christian missionaries visiting in his area and went to see them. As soon as they told him about Jesus, he knew *this* was the one true God he'd been waiting to meet.

On another occasion, I was privileged to travel to Shabwalala, a small dusty town 100 miles outside of the capital of Zambia. As I was standing in a field talking with a group of African boys, we heard a clanging noise slowly coming down the nearby path. I turned to find a rail-thin cow with a bell around its neck. An old, disheveled-looking man was leading it down the road with a frayed rope. The man immediately came up to me and began rattling off words in his native Bebma dialect as if I understood him. Obviously, I didn't, so I turned to my translator, Abel Tembo, for the story . . .

"This man has walked a day and a half to meet with you," Abel relayed. "He heard there were white missionaries from America visiting, and he has a question he wants to ask you."

When I asked Abel about the cow, he said the man couldn't leave his only cow behind or it would be stolen, so he brought it all the way with him. As Abel was telling me this, the man began to point up at the sky and around him while rattling off more unfamiliar words.

"I know there's a god," he said to me through Abel, "because all of this had to come from somewhere. It couldn't have come from nothing. But I don't know where to take it from there . . ."

I nearly burst into tears. Here was a man nearing the end of his life, certainly weathered by its trials and storms. He obviously had little to eat, maybe wasn't even sure where his next meal was going to come from. And yet the burning inside him had caused him to leave everything at the chance that maybe a strange foreigner might have an answer to his soul-searing question.

This was probably the most intelligent man I've ever met—more so than any of the university professors I was used to meeting on American campuses—because he knew enough about what he *didn't know* to seek out an answer. He recognized the stark contrast between the fullness of his surroundings and the emptiness inside him.

It was a matter of words before he accepted Jesus into his heart.

"I have sought this for my whole life," he said with tears in his eyes, his life changed forever and the weight of the world lifted off his shoulders. He then asked if I would come to his village. "There are 13 more who need to know this," he pleaded. We went and saw 13 more souls added to the kingdom of God.

Lost and Found

I don't tell these stories to lather up an emotional response. I tell them because they are proof of a truth that all of us, at our core, already know. Having been to the "Africas" of this world, to the farthest regions and most remote places, I can say this having experienced it: People know God. They also know their dire need for Him. Romans 1:20 says of these people, "Since the creation of the world His invisible attributes are clearly seen, being understood by the things that are made, even His eternal power and Godhead, so that they are without excuse."

He may be known by a different name. He may even be shown in a different manner. But God has been revealed to all souls, no matter where or how. And those who will honestly seek Him will honestly find Him. Nobody goes to hell because they couldn't be reached; they go because they didn't want God. The wonderful news is that anyone who wants God will find Him.

"And you will seek Me and find Me, when you search for Me with all your heart. I will be found by you" (Jer. 29:13-14).

The truth of Christianity is not contingent upon how many have or have not heard. Likewise, the truth of hell isn't dependent upon whether the noble savage in the jungle or your atheist neighbor receives Jesus as Lord. Hell still exists, whether one person is headed there or a trillion. And the Bible still defines that salvation—the way to avoid hell—is through Jesus only.

That kind of puts a different spin on the fiery afterlife, doesn't it? Rather than causing us to react with indifference, the reality of hell should serve as a mandate for missions. With one word—*Jesus*—we can be a part of lifting the burden of souls in anguish. We can depopulate hell!

Response

Reasons to accept the reality of hell:

Testimony of the Bible
Warnings of Jesus
Recognition by the Church
Morally appropriate
Logically necessary
Unchanged by our biases

People Are Basically Good

Common Objection:
"I don't think I'm a sinner. I'm not so bad."

In October 2005, media wire services reported an exceptionally heinous crime. In the small town of Kittanning, Pennsylvania, neighbors Peggy Jo Conner and Valerie Oskin were fast becoming close friends, as both were supposedly expecting babies. But on October 14, Conner beat Oskin with a baseball bat, dragged her into a wooded area and sliced open her abdomen in an attempt to steal Oskin's baby.

Later medical tests revealed that Conner was not actually pregnant, and there was no evidence that she had been—though she had bought a bassinette, baby swing and other baby items in anticipation of having a new baby. The 38-year-old Conner had three kids of her own, but she reportedly wanted another child and it was her jealousy that motivated her to beat Oskins and attempt to take her eight-month-old fetus.

Amazingly, this crime, described as "grotesque" by legal and medical personnel, was interrupted by a 17-year-old boy who, while driving his all-terrain vehicle through the woods, saw the crime and alerted the police. It was just short of a miracle that Oskin survived the beating and her baby was delivered by emergency C-section. The teenage boy was called a hero. Had he come by even a few moments later, the victims would probably not have lived. On ABC's *Good Morning America*, Kittanning district attorney Scott Andreassi said, "If anyone was looking for a reason to believe in a higher power, this is it. If that 17-year-old young man had not come along when he did, [Mrs. Oskins] would have bled to death."[1]

News of the Day

After decades of relative peace, Toowoomba, Australia, a quiet provincial city known for its farming population, was rocked by four grisly murders. In 2002, a 25-year-old mother was sexually assaulted, strangled and left hanged on a tree in the inner city. In 2004, two teenagers brutally murdered an 86-year-old war veteran. And in January 2006, a 76-year-old man and his 73-year-old wife were both stabbed to death in their kitchen by a man believed to have been living with the couple.[2]

In the Philippines, four teenagers were arrested after gang-raping two 15-year-old girls in a sugarcane plantation. The girls, who wanted to be part of the boy's social club, had been told they were being initiated into the group.[3]

Columbian police apprehended a man who is believed to have murdered 29 children, at least half of whom were under the age of 10. Their bones were found strewn over two separate burial sites, and most of the skeletons were incomplete.[4]

In Kuwait, Adnan Al-Enezi blindfolded and handcuffed his own 13-year-old daughter, sliced her throat once, then used a sharper blade as she screamed in pain—all while forcing the girl's two brothers and sister to watch. The reason? Al-Enezi thought the girl wasn't a virgin. Forensic examinations proved she was.[5]

Had Enough?

It's enough to make you nauseated, isn't it? Yet this is the type of news we hear every day. Of course, it's become cliché to use real-world cases like these as an example of the signs of the times, or even to show the reign of evil in this world. In fact, some of you may have glossed over the last few paragraphs, thinking that you've heard one preacher too many do the same thing to hammer home an overworked point. *Yeah, yeah . . . this world's going to hell in a handbasket. We know.*

Or do we? I'm beginning to have my doubts. Especially when I hear countless people try to pronounce their "goodness" by excluding themselves from the rest of the world. *"I'm not that bad. It's not like I've murdered or raped anyone, you know. I don't drink. Don't smoke. I've never even cursed in my entire life."*

It's amazing what we'll come up with to make ourselves look good. Thirty years of perfect church attendance. Singing on the worship team every Sunday. Volunteering once a month at a nearby nursing home. Sometimes we even expect to earn honors for how our kids turn out. Sorry if I'm bursting your bubble, but as wonderful as those things are, they don't change your soul one bit. In fact, they won't ever change one fundamental fact: You're still bad.

Exclusion Denied

There is not a righteous man on earth who does what is right and never sins.
Ecclesiastes 7:20, *NIV*

All we like sheep have gone astray; we have turned, every one, to his own way.
Isaiah 53:6

For all have sinned and fall short of the glory of God.
Romans 3:23

Without rehashing the validity of the Bible—without explaining as we've already done why God's Word is indeed the ultimate truth—let me remind you of this: God says we're sinful. That means we're sinful. Case closed.

Why isn't this up for debate? Because God, by definition, is holiness. It's who He is. And if anyone can see a dirty spot on snow-white linen, it's Him. God can't stand sin because there isn't a drop of sin within His nature. In fact, His "inability" to tolerate sin led Him to sacrifice His only Son just to have our sins wiped clean. He abhors the fact that our natural state is one that completely opposes who He is, and yet He made a way for that to change.

Notice, however, that it's not a matter of being "not so bad" or "pretty good." God does not rank our sinfulness—a matter that infuriates the proud among us. It's a humbling—no, make that outrageous—thought to realize that in the grand perspective of sin there is no difference between a murderer and a three-year-old who lies to Mommy about having brushed her teeth before going to bed. To our fleshly pride, that's downright insulting, isn't it?! Because ultimately, it means we can *never* do enough good in God's eyes to get us out of the dungeon of sinfulness. And yet nothing could be truer.

"No sin is small. No grain of sand is small in the mechanism of a watch."

—Jeremy Taylor, bishop and theologian

All the Same

What's ironic is how the world's moral relativism mirrors this aspect of our naturally sinful state. Recall the story that opened this chapter. In a world without moral absolutes, the actions of Peggy Jo Conner and the 17-year-old boy who rescued the other woman are qualitatively the same. If there is no objective standard of right and wrong existing apart from human opinion or preference, then it makes no sense to condemn one set of motives and actions as wrong and to praise another as being virtuous. There would be no "good vs. evil"; it would all just be "stuff that happened." In other words, a would-be murderer such as Conner would be on the same level as the teenage hero.

"It is as supreme folly to talk of a little sin, as it would be to talk of a small Decalogue that forbids it, or a diminutive God that hates it, or a shallow hell that shall punish it."
—Charles Seymour Robinson, American clergyman and author[7]

When it comes to sin, that's not such a crazy idea. Because even the "heroes" among us hold evil within their hearts. Even the Mother Teresas and Brother Andrews are sinful. How do I know? Remember the example we used at the beginning of this book regarding the 10 separate islands? In each case, the completely separated people groups shared similar values. (And recall that C. S. Lewis and several other apologists have analyzed similar scenarios throughout cultural history.) They upheld virtues such as kindness, love and honesty. They looked down on murdering, stealing, lying, cheating and the like.

The point is not that we've all followed the same moral code for all time. My point is that we all intuitively *know* what's right and wrong (see Gen. 2:17; 3:6). Since the Fall, the knowledge of good and evil has been innately within us. And, given the choice, *all of us*—declare both the Bible and all of human history—will choose wrong. No matter how hard we try not to mess up, we will. And no matter how vigorously we attempt to reform ourselves, we can't.

Opportunity Rises From the Ashes

Thankfully, the story doesn't end there. I'd be doing a disservice to the character of God if I only relayed the message of our utter sinfulness. Because somehow, some way, in the midst of our seemingly permanent and irrecoverable evil, God's holy light penetrated through. Our hero came to save the day. Check that—He saved eternity.

We've mentioned that in His righteousness, God cannot stand sin. But we should never forget that in His love, God has promised us that He will not part from us. And because of that, He risked the pain and shame that was heaped on His most beloved—His Son, Jesus—so that we could be just as permanently loved as Jesus. In Christ, we can become spotless, which gives us the right to join Him for eternity—perfectly pure and acceptable to a Holy Father.

Summary Response

Reasons to admit personal guilt and spiritual need:

The clarity of the Bible
The presence of conscience
The guilt throughout cultures
The inability of human reform
The reality of punishment
The assessment of Jesus
The historicity of the cross

Christians Are All Hypocrites

Common Objection:
"I'd be interested in Christ if it weren't for the Christians. Why would I want to become one of them?"

I've spent most of this book refuting objections, saying why they are not true. But this one—well, I have to admit there's a lot of truth in it. Many Christians—perhaps all Christians—are hypocrites. We don't live up to our highest aspirations for ourselves. And we certainly don't live up to the standard that God set for us in Scripture, or the standard that Jesus lived.

And church scandals aren't just a twenty-first-century thing, you know. Throughout all history, Christianity has had more than its share of leaders who badly misrepresent the faith. Thanks in no small part to the false piety of a corrupt Church, the world sees Christianity as just another religion, just another lifestyle option—but one whose followers have no particular spiritual power aren't particularly different in character and love from the followers of most other religions.

Guilty as Charged

Again, there is some truth to this accusation of hypocrisy. You don't have to look far to see that most Christians don't live up to the standard Jesus set. For example, Jesus told a rich young man who was satisfied with his wealth, position and piety, "Sell what you have and give to the poor, and you will have treasure in heaven; and come, follow Me" (Matt. 19:21). He told another, who wanted to bury his father before he followed Jesus, to "let the dead bury the dead." In fact, those of us who promote family values might find it hard to take these words of Jesus: "He who loves father or mother more than Me is not worthy of Me. And he who loves son or daughter more than Me is not worthy of Me. And he who does not take his cross and follow after Me is not worthy of Me" (Matt. 10:37-38).

What was Jesus' point? His point was that following Him requires *everything*.

It's not hard to find plenty of examples from history of Christians—or at least those who claim to be Christians—behaving badly. Let's take a look at a couple of the most notorious historical blunders that cause the most problems for unbelievers.

"The time is coming that whoever kills you will think that he offers God service. And these things they will do to you because they have not known the Father nor Me" (John 16:2-3).

The Crusades

Toss out the phrase "religious hypocrisy" and most likely the first reaction you get will involve the medieval Crusades. A common response sounds something like this: "If Christianity is so great, then why is it responsible for so many not-so-great things?" Or sometimes it is a more general response: "Some of the great atrocities of history have been committed in the name of religion."

Before we look at a few historical facts—and my explanations—about the Crusades, it is important to consider a couple of overarching principles. First of all, as we have already discussed, the behavior of individuals or even large groups of Christians neither proves nor disproves the truth of Christianity. I hate to reduce this argument to a bumper sticker, but there is truth in the one that says, "Christians aren't perfect, just forgiven." I will be the first to admit that when Christians behave badly, we are not providing a good witness of the transforming power of Jesus—but we are providing a good example of the need for and the extent of His forgiveness!

Second, it is important to remember—again, as we have already discussed—that not everything in the history books is true. As it turns out, much of what we think we know about the Crusades is either wrong or incomplete.

The Crusades began around A.D. 1100, a full millennium after Jesus walked on the earth. During those 1,000-plus years, Christianity grew remarkably. It grew because of the missionary zeal of many Early Church leaders, but it also grew because of the quiet and good lives of many followers. During the Roman Empire in the first two centuries after Christ, for example, abortion and infanticide were common. Christians, appalled by these practices, took in the often female children who were being killed—and they took them into their families in large numbers. Rodney Stark, in his book *The Rise of Christianity*, records that by the end of the second century A.D., because of the love and care that Christians showed for each other, their life spans were longer, their families were bigger and the growth of the Church was almost as much a demographic phenomenon as an evangelistic phenomenon.

But as Christianity grew, it also grew in economic and political power. And as Islam grew in the Middle East, there came an almost inevitable clash of civilizations. Add to this the fact that many of Jesus' teachings were distorted. The leaders of the Roman and Eastern churches—forgetting that Jesus' kingdom is "not of this world" were in a struggle for power and money.

In the midst of the complicated historical mix, we add the fact that in those days—as today—it was common for Christians to make pilgrimages to the Holy Land. The spread of Islam, and the increased control of many regions in the Middle East by Muslims, brought these Christians into conflict. These journeys were often prevented. Christians were killed. And the leaders of the Christian Church, who were by this time in control of military forces, were mobilized.

At their core, in other words, the Crusades weren't about spreading the Good News. That's not to say there weren't honorable motives involved. Defending the lives of Christian pilgrims was certainly worth doing. Keeping the Middle East open and free for travel and commerce were certainly laudable goals. But it is also important to admit that for many leaders on both sides, the Crusades were about taking control of land for personal gain. Motives got mixed and the idea of defending pilgrims quickly turned into cultural imperialism.

The conflict came to a head in 1071 at the Battle of Manzikert near Armenia. There Seljuk Turks (Muslims from Central Asia) fought and defeated Byzantine Christians. In response to this, and with full support from the Pope, the Crusades were launched, the first commencing in 1096.[1] After initial successes and a century of Christian rule in Jerusalem, Saladin the Great amassed his Muslim forces for the Battle of Hatin, which occurred on July 5, 1187. In the battle, Saladin's forces decimated the Christian army and eventually conquered the city of Jerusalem (fighting on or near the hill where Christ had preached the Sermon on the Mount). On that day, more than 30,000 Christian soldiers were killed.

It seemed that spearheading bloody crusades and military initiatives were not among the things Christ had commissioned His Church to do.

Is Religion the Root of Wrong?

Even though it could be argued, at least in part, that the Crusades were cultural self-defense (this is not to excuse all the atrocities or the attacks against Jews and Eastern Christians), clearly the Crusades are an embarrassment to any modern-day believer. Is it possible for a Christian to defend the atrocities that took place during the Crusades? Not at all. But let's take a look at some of the side issues that must be taken into account.

In the case of the Crusades, it's not certain that many of the crusaders were truly born-again believers. Their behavior certainly can't be considered normal for those earnestly following Jesus' teachings.

Of course, all religious zealots—including the leaders of the Crusades—say theirs is the true religion. The Bible, however, has its own definition of true religion: "Pure and undefiled religion before God the Father is this: to visit orphans and widows in their trouble" (Jas. 1:27).

This definition implies humility and a care for what some have called "the least and the lost." Scripture teaches us not to pursue status, position, wealth or power—but to follow Jesus, the Suffering Servant.

God's definition of true religion is not the same as the definition that we have learned from a slanted view of history, or even what most religious leaders want us to believe. That brand of religion isn't the same thing as the true religion that springs from a relationship with Christ.

In fact, it's often quite the opposite. We see in the Bible that Jesus offered grace and words of love to everyone but one group of people: the ultra-religious. The Pharisees and Sadducees, who were called a "brood of vipers" (Matt. 3:7), were pompous religious zealots so caught up in ritual that they were of no good on Earth. Rituals are not the same as reality—and Jesus is all about bringing His kingdom into our reality. No other group received such harsh warnings as these guys, and yet to the end they refused to look past their own works and recognize Jesus for who He is.

In fact, the word "religion" comes from the joining of two Latin words and is related to the concept of "healing of a broken ligament." Think of a cast on a broken bone; it's an *external* bandage designed to heal an *internal* wound. For an orthopedist treating a sprain or break, this is fine. But for an unregenerate sinner needing to become rightly related to God, it's not. As we talked about in the last chapter, humanity's problem is internal. It's an unsaved condition of spiritual deadness—sin—into which we are all born. Religion is the name we give to any of a million approaches to make amends for this state and put ourselves right with God. Religion, then, is something we *do*. Christianity, on the other hand, is about something that has been *done*. Religious activities are about man reaching up to heaven. But the Good News of Christianity is the story of Jesus coming down from heaven to reach Earth.

Whenever we see the atrocious deeds of zealots claiming to act in the name of God, we can infer that there has been a lack of the true spiritual birth that Jesus spoke of in John 3. Religion is about *outward works*. Christianity is about an *inward personal relationship* initiated by repentance and faith (see Eph. 2:8-10; 2 Cor. 5:17; Titus 3:11). When that relationship truly directs every decision in life, results such as the Crusades are a virtual impossibility.

Facing the Facts

As a person who has studied Christianity and the history of world religions for two decades, I'm uncomfortable with much of the current media coverage given to religious issues. Two things trouble me in particular. I object to the fact that biblical

Christianity is often considered on the same plane with aberrant, often violent, religions. Further, I balk at the way people in America and the West are being misled, as we are incessantly told, "Islam is a religion of peace. This otherwise great religion has been marred by the actions of a radical minority. The true teachings of Islam are actually peaceful."

Is Islam truly a religion of peace, one that promotes civility? Consider the research of noted historian Samuel P. Huntington, who states, "Protests against anti-Western violence have been totally absent in Muslim countries. Muslim governments have been strikingly reticent when it comes to condemning terrorist attacks against the West."[2] Huntington is a Harvard University professor of history, an expert on international studies, has been president of the American Political Science Association, and served in the cabinet of the Carter administration. Criticized by the media and some academics for entitling one section in his book "Islam's Bloody Borders," he explains his rationale:

> Wherever one looks along the perimeter of Islam, Muslims have problems living peaceably with their neighbors. Muslims make up about one-fifth of the world's population, but in the 1990s, they have been far more involved in inter-group violence than the people of any other civilization. The evidence is overwhelming . . . There were, in short, three times as many intercivilizational conflicts involving Muslims as there were conflicts between all non-Muslim civilizations. Islam's borders are bloody, and so are its innards.[3]

Years before the 9/11 attacks and the more recent Islamic violence, former president Jimmy Carter, a man known for his normally gentle demeanor, observed, "The Islamic world is torn by strife that is not limited to combat with Israel. Iran and Iraq's conflict demonstrates Islam's love for bloodshed and warfare."[4]

The anti-blasphemy laws of Islamic-led Pakistan mean death for anyone who speaks against Muhammad or the Koran. In Sudan, Islamic leaders have killed millions of Christians and made slaves of countless others. These practices are going on today, though media outlets and journalists have done little to share this with the American viewing public.

Many Islamic countries allow little or no freedom for their citizens and impose severe penalties (even death) for conversion to another religion. *Newsweek* reported that "prospects for democracy in the Islamic world are dim. Islamic countries allowing citizens little or no civil rights include: Morocco, Bahrain, United Arab Emirates, Lebanon, Egypt, Iran, Yemen, Saudi Arabia, Libya, Syria and Iraq. (These major Islamic countries are described as 'stifled,' with basic rights denied by corrupt governments and any organized opposition usually murdered.)"[5]

Why do I feel the need to point out these unpopular facts? First, because few others seem to be doing so. For whatever reason, the "offend none but the Christians" media refuses to portray Islam in a negative light, despite centuries' worth of facts. But in addition, it helps shed some light on the two-sided coin of the Crusades. In describing the vast differences between Christianity and Islam, Norm Geisler said this:

> In the early days of Christianity, you might be killed for becoming a Christian. In the early days of Islam's growth, you might be killed for not becoming a Muslim! In other words, the spread of these two monotheistic faiths could not have been more different: Islam spread by using the sword on others; Christianity spread when others used the sword on it.[6]

Adding Fuel to the Fire

The fundamental principle of Christianity is love. The fundamental principle of Islam is upholding the name of Allah and submitting to Islamic law, even if that requires killing others in the name of *jihad* (though of course, not all Muslims become *Jihad* Muslims; many are looking for a way out of the *jihadi* mentality). Does that change the fact that Christians went around slaughtering Muslims and holding a sword to the necks of countless innocent civilians in an attempt to convert them? Not one bit. Both Christians and Muslims should be held in contempt for their unjustifiable actions.

The same can be said of Adolph Hitler, who some say was a Christian because of his early ambitions to be a priest. Because Hitler committed genocide against the Jews and was responsible for countless other atrocities, many of these same people say that Christianity is therefore atrocious and blameworthy. Some have even claimed that his was a "Christian regime," and that the Third Reich provides a glimpse of what a country would look like if Christians had their way in the government.

However, it is clear that Hitler was indeed not a Christian. Both his words—he once said, "Christianity is an invention of sick brains; one could imagine nothing more senseless"[7]—and his despicably un-Christlike actions settle the case. U.S. Justice Robert Jackson, who was the chief prosecutor at the 1947 postwar Nuremburg Trials, pointed out, "The Nazi Party always was predominantly anti-Christian in its ideology." He added that Hitler had "carried out a systematic and relentless repression of all Christian sects and churches."[8]

Those Nuremburg Trials also unfolded an interesting issue that we've already discussed. Jackson claimed the Nazis were guilty of "moral as well as legal wrong," and appealed to the universal "moral sense of mankind" in contending that Hitler and his cohorts had violated an objective moral law higher than the Nazis' own self-initiated laws.[9] In desiring to eradicate the Jews and in murdering millions, they had transgressed a moral standard that all of humanity would recognize.

This once again proves that the nature of morality is *absolute* or fixed. Morals are objective and absolute because they are based on the character of God, which is fixed and unchanging. If morals were *subjective* or simply dreamed up only by minds (and whims) of humans, then it would make no sense to praise one action as noble and condemn another as evil. If the world had no solid ethical moorings (i.e., absolute truths), then the actions of Hitler or Osama bin Laden would be no different than those of Billy Graham.

"I like your Christ, I do not like your Christians. Your Christians are so unlike your Christ."

—Mahatma Gandhi

Human Condition

What does any of this have to do with the poor example Christians have set for centuries? My point is this: As stated in the previous chapter, humans are inherently sinful. We're full of potential wickedness and unimaginable evil. Neither Christianity nor Islam can save us from that because both are mere religions that emphasize works. And works combined with religious zeal, as history shows, only amounts to atrocities. Only one thing—one person—can save us from our sinful state: Jesus Christ.

Are Christians hypocrites? You bet. Have they caused a permanent stain on history and therefore tainted the gospel?

Without a doubt. Are you bound to face a few other Christians in your life who will make you want to do anything but become a Christian? Uh-huh. But let me follow those questions up with these: Are non-Christians hypocrites? Have non-Christians caused a permanent stain on history? Are there non-Christians today who badly misrepresent a cause they claim to represent?

When it comes to being screw-ups, we're all in the same boat—Christians and non-Christians. We all have failed and continue to fail miserably. Labeling yourself as a Christian doesn't change much without actually following through with what it means to be a Christian. And *that's* the very problem Christianity has had throughout its existence. Like a leech that won't let go, true Christianity has been unable to shake the "religion" that ruins its name.

So if history shows that Christians have messed up just as badly as non-Christians, why would anyone ever want to become a Christ-follower? Because of this simple fact: Just because there are poor examples of Christ doesn't mean Christ is like those representations. Humans are born to err. Once again, it's our sinful nature. By contrast, Jesus Christ never once sinned. He redeemed our sinful nature by His death on the cross. The existence of the counterfeit does not negate the reality of the genuine. In other words, just because we see a lot of "counterfeit" Christ-followers doesn't in the slightest way change the truth that Jesus is the real deal.

Thankfully, we don't invite Christians into our heart. We invite Christ, who is most certainly *not* a hypocrite! Likewise, we don't refer to the words and actions of Christians as our standards; we look only to Jesus' words and actions. He set the bar— no one else. For some reason, He chose to be represented on this earth by His people, the Church. He called them Christians—followers of Christ. If you have accepted Him as Lord and Savior of your life, then you bear His name. That means you are His representative, His ambassador. What you do, think and say defines how others view Him and have a profound affect on their eternal destination. That's a scary thought, now isn't it? Yet that's the reality of Christianity.

"The church is the only organization that exists almost solely for the benefit of its non-members."

—Anonymous

Because of that, how much more should we as Christians point to the relationship we can have with Christ rather than to the rituals of normal religion? It is that element that sets Christianity apart from any other faith. We don't claim to have it all right. We've certainly messed up and continue to do so. But thankfully, by God's redeeming grace, we will continue to point to the source of all perfection, Jesus Christ. And He will never fail.

Summary Response

Reasons to believe Christianity despite
the behavior of some Christians:

Because God offers you Christ, not Christians
Because Christian truth is not negated by human failures
Because in reality, all people are hypocrites
Because our need for Jesus is all the more clear

A Merciful God Wouldn't Allow Suffering

Common Objection:
"Why is there evil in the world?
What about suffering?"

"How can you say that God is loving and good when there's so much evil and suffering in the world?" As the college student's question echoed in the auditorium, an audience of several hundred people silently awaited my answer. The questioner had more: "I mean, if God is all-powerful as Christians say, why doesn't He fix the world? *Can* He? Or does God not care?"

Ah, the problem of pain. It's a perennial issue for the defender of Christianity, and rightfully so. It's also a big question, deserving of a substantive answer. For the Christian apologist, it boils down to this: How are we to reconcile what we believe about God (that He is all-powerful, good, wise, loving, just and merciful) with the undeniable realities of sin, death, evil, pain, injustice and evil in this world?

A supremely perfect Creator and grossly fallen world appear to be two irreconcilable concepts. But the problem of evil doesn't nullify the claims of Christianity. In other words, just because suffering exists doesn't mean God is any less loving or good—unless, of course, God is the source of that suffering or evil.

It will probably come as no surprise to you that my position is that He is *not* the source of evil. He allows evil and suffering and pain, but He does not cause it. The question, then, is who does?

Either God wants to abolish evil, and cannot;
or He can, but does not want to;
or He cannot and does not want to.
If He wants to, but cannot, He is impotent.
If He can, but does not want to, He is wicked.
But if God both can and wants to abolish evil,
then how come evil is in the world?

—*Epicurus*

Then Who Caused the Current Catastrophes?

Every year seems to bring with it a new round of seemingly unexplainable disasters. In 2005, in the aftermath of the worst tsunami in human history and an onslaught of deadly hurricanes (Katrina, Rita and Wilma), many were asking, "Where is God? Why did God do this?" Once again, in other words: If God is so powerful, why didn't He control the waves? If He's so wise, wouldn't He have known beforehand? And if He's so full of love, why did He allow it?

Before directly addressing those questions, let's acknowledge the reality of our present condition: We live in a fallen world. God made the world perfect, and He made us without sin. But He gave us a choice. Adam made the wrong choice, and we now live in the world that his bad choice created.

Now, it is perfectly reasonable to ask this question: Why? Why did God give us that choice? We will never fully know, this side of eternity, the answer to that question. It is truly a tough question. In fact, the great evangelical Christian theologian John Stott wrote, "The fact of suffering undoubtedly constitutes the single greatest challenge to the Christian faith."

But even with our incomplete knowledge, we have an inkling of the answer to that question: If God did not give us that choice, we would never really be fully human or fully made in the image of God.

There is much, then, that we can say about the problem of evil. People who have thought about this problem deeply say there are two types of evils in this world. First, there is *moral* evil (sin, murder, theft, rape, war, carnage, and so forth.). These are direct "expressions," if you will, of our sinful state. But there are also *natural* evils (disasters, accidents, calamities in the physical world), all of which are the results of that moral evil. In other words, the moral evil that we committed was such an affront to God's created order that it affected even the operation of the universe. That man is sometimes brought to calamity by these effects is a natural and logical consequence of the disorder that now plays a role in the universe.

Think about the weather patterns we see on a daily basis and how these might be connected to our disobedience. You'll recall the account of Adam and Eve's choice to sin against God in the Garden of Eden (see Gen. 3). Later on, the world had become so evil that God judged the human race through a worldwide cataclysmic flood (see Gen. 7-10). During and after the Flood, the earth's plates shifted and crumbled, and its climate was drastically altered. Through the family of faithful Noah, the human race was spared and the planet's population was once again replenished. But in the post-Flood world, earthquakes still occur, as does the annual cycle of tropical depressions, hurricanes and tornados.

Does God cause every storm? Not really. From the first hint of lightning following the flood of Noah, the earth's weather has simply followed the pattern of humanity's sin. Some have even surmised that the recent increase in violent weather reflects the increase in our sinfulness. Statistically speaking, the damage from recent hurricanes could have been much worse. According to NASA, though, the United States has the world's most violent weather. In a typical year, the U.S. experiences some 10,000 violent thunderstorms, 5,000 floods of varying sizes, 1,000 tornadoes and, as we know all too well, numerous hurricanes.[1]

With this in mind, it's a wonder that more places aren't severely damaged by weather, or that more lives aren't lost. Rather than *blame* God, it's probably more suitable to *praise* God, given the data, and ask, "How is it that the human race is so protected and shielded, given the self-inflicted dangers posed to humans by this world?" We cannot forget that humanity—not God—is to blame for natural evil. It was our sinfulness that caused God to curse the earth (see Gen. 3:17). As Romans 8:21-22 points out, the world is in bondage and is suffering from man-induced "corruption."

God did not create the world this way. His intent wasn't to have a fallen creation—neither man nor nature. When God looked over all that He had created, He saw that it was good (see Gen. 1:10), and when God thinks something is good, you can know that it's *perfectly* good. But in our sinfulness, humanity chose to rebel against God, which ushered in sin and death, and in the process also caused chaos throughout the earth.

A Solution in Sight

God will eventually make the world new again. Revelation 21:4 promises that "God will wipe away every tear from their eyes; there shall be no more death, nor sorrow, nor crying. There shall be no more pain." Right now, we're still shedding tears. There is death, sorrow, crying and pain. The late preacher Dr. Vance H.

Coming to Grips with the Reality of Evil: Five Available Options

1. *Atheism:* There is no God.

2. *Dualism:* Good and evil are really the same thing—yin and yang, forever in a cosmic dance—just different sides of the same coin.

3. *Illusionism:* Maybe what I think is evil is only *maya,* illusion. Maybe nothing is *truly* bad . . . or good; maybe stuff just is. Many (though not all) Eastern religions hold this worldview.

4. *Finite god-ism:* Maybe God would like to rid the world of evil but somehow isn't able. He is finite, or has limits. Indeed, perhaps one of those limits is that He is not all good, that evil is a part of His character.

5. *Trinitarian Monotheism:* God exists and is good, wise and all-powerful. Though evil is now present, the universe will be rid of it one day. In fact, God has, through His Son, victoriously addressed the problem already.

Havner (who was highly influential in Billy Graham's life) was renowned for his take on a Hungarian proverb: "Adam and Eve bit the apple, and our teeth still ache." This proverb actually has a biblical basis. Ezekiel 18:2 says, "The fathers eat sour grapes, and the children's teeth are set on edge." Indeed, we feel the ache on a regular basis—with each news flash that reports the latest tragedy. The ripple effect of sin touches every life, every family and every culture.

I'll be the first to admit that the explanation of evil I've offered is not complete. As I said earlier, suffering and evil are so devastating to us as individuals, to us as humans, and—even—to the very order of the created universe, that we want an ultimate and complete answer. But just as we can't fully explain the heights of God's love, neither can we fully explain the depth of sin and evil. Indeed, part of the mystery of God's love for us is that it more than covers our sin and the suffering in the world. It gives meaning to the suffering.

Indeed, more than any other belief system, Christianity addresses the origin and presence of evil while also offering hope in the eventual eradication of all pain. Unlike Eastern religions, Christianity doesn't deny that evil is real. It's uniquely positioned to offer hope and meaning. In Christianity, we can understand *how* evil came to be (the temptation of Satan and the fall of man; see Genesis 3). We can accept the fact of our guilt, but we can also rest in the promise of God's solution, which involves His unfathomable love.

Think about it: To accomplish our salvation, *the Creator allowed Himself to be murdered by His creation.* Obviously, that doesn't make sense to our limited understanding, just as it doesn't make sense that a loving God would allow pain and suffering. Yet through Jesus' victory over sin, death, evil and the grave, the world's healing is conclusively guaranteed. It's as if God says, "Trust me, world . . . if I can rise from the grave and conquer death, be assured that I am able to conquer any problem you are facing!"

Instinctively Right

The realities of sin and evil are certainly not solved by reverting to skepticism or atheism. Again, just because you refuse to acknowledge God doesn't change the fact that bad things happen in this world. The amazingly insightful C. S. Lewis put it this way: "A man can no more diminish God's glory by refusing to worship Him than a lunatic can put out the sun by scribbling the word *darkness* on his cell."[2] Our inborn, innate rational faculties (what your grandmother called "common sense") tell us that there must be a God, that God must be good, and that good will win in the end.

We intuitively know that good is better than bad. We're born with a keen sense of justice. All you have to do to figure that one out is watch a group of children around the table at a picnic: "He took my cookie! Make him give it back!" The desire to see justice served is universal. And deep in their hearts, most people believe that God will, in the end, justly iron out all of the world's wrinkles. For example, taking comfort in his knowledge of God, Abraham asked, "Shall not the Judge of all the earth do right?" (Gen. 18:25).

We can securely place our hope in the fact that God is in control and that He will, at least someday, make everything right. With that, our comfort lies in knowing that in His Word, God has promised to do precisely these things . . . and more.

"There is no learning sympathy except by suffering. It cannot be studied from a book, it must be written on the heart. You must go through the fire if you would have sympathy for others who tread glowing coals. You must yourself bear the cross if you would feel for those whose life is a burden to them."

—*Charles H. Spurgeon*[3]

But Why Must the Innocent Suffer?

This is a question that brings to mind the issue of God sending to hell those who have never heard His name before. In a previous chapter, we referred to this as the Africa question. Its answer lies in the truth that all humans are inherently sinful, that we innately know the difference between right and wrong, and that—without prompting by the Holy Spirit—we'll always choose to go against God.

For the question of the innocent suffering, the answer is the same. First, we must recognize the error in calling anyone truly innocent. We do this according to our standards of goodness—not God's. God is not only completely righteous, but He is also the only one worthy of judging who is innocent and who isn't; and He has already deemed all of humanity guilty because of our sin. The Bible says that everyone—even those we call innocent—has sinned and egregiously missed God's intended standard, which is holiness (see Rom. 3:23). Thus, we have a twofold problem: We inherited the sinful nature of Adam, and we commit sinful deeds on our own. We know the right, yet do the wrong. We are guilty.

The only truly innocent person who ever lived was Jesus. Jesus was perfect and sinless, deserving of worship and praise, yet was rejected and killed. The righteous Jesus suffered on the cross for guilty humanity. As theologian Dorothy Sayers writes:

> For whatever reason God chose to make man as he is—limited and suffering and subject to sorrows and death—He had the honesty and courage to take His own medicine . . . He has Himself gone through the whole of human experience, from the trivial irritations of family life and the cramping restrictions of hard work and lack of money to the worst horrors of pain and humiliation, defeat, despair and death. When He was a man, He played the man. He was born in poverty and died in disgrace, and thought it well worthwhile.[4]

> *"Reflect upon your present blessings,*
> *Of which every person has many;*
> *Not upon your past misfortunes,*
> *Of which all have some."*
> —*Charles Dickens*[5]

Still, some may be stuck at that seemingly unconquerable question—*Why?* Before we demand that God give an accounting, we must gently remind ourselves that all suffering is ultimately self-inflicted. Our free will is the origin of pain, suffering and the entry point for sin into this world. The original humans used their moral faculties—choice, will, volition—to rebel against God. However, the obligation is on us to praise Jesus Christ for enacting a solution; the obligation is not on God to apologize to us.

God, however, mercifully does two things for us in relation to our questions about suffering. He has graciously disclosed enough information to help us process our grief appropriately. God has told us where sin came from, its unfortunate results and how evil will finally and fully be banished one day. Christ's empty grave is an incredibly comforting promise from God that essentially reminds us that He is in control. We can safely trust Him.

Not only has God given us knowledge of our pain and a reminder of His sovereignty, but He has also given us hope and purpose.

Pain for a Purpose

If we accept that the results of evil—pain, suffering and death—are not from God, yet He allows them, then we must assume that they play a part in His plan. And since we know that His plan is one of eternal redemption—that the world will be saved—then it's safe to say that pain must play a role in our personal redemption. Pain indeed has a purpose.

In what has become his trademark quote, C. S. Lewis observed that the challenges and the pains of life are tools by which God can get our attention: "God whispers to us in our pleasures, speaks in our conscience, but shouts in our pains: It is His megaphone to rouse a deaf world."[6]

For a non-Christian, this may seem ridiculous. And yet it may be that suffering is the only means by which the nonbeliever will see his need for Christ. Only God knows. Meanwhile, believers who suffer can emerge from their valleys with purified character, deeper faith and a greater awareness of how truly faithful God is. For those who subscribe to Lewis's statement, the important thing is to remember that God is loving and merciful even when trials and sufferings are permitted to come into our lives: "And we know that God causes everything to work together for the good of those who love God and are called according to His purpose for them" (Rom. 8:28, *NLT*).

20 Reasons Why God Allows Suffering in the World

1. Suffering uncovers what is really inside of our hearts.
2. Suffering breaks us of our pride.
3. Suffering can deepen our desire for God.
4. Suffering can mature us.
5. Suffering can breed humility.
6. Suffering may be a warning of something potentially *worse*.
7. Suffering can jump-start our prayer life.

8. Suffering may prompt a lost person to receive Christ.

9. Suffering may lead a Christian to confess sin.

10. Suffering helps us deepen our trust in God.

11. Suffering can deepen our appreciation for Scripture.

12. Suffering helps us appreciate other Christians who were victorious.

13. Suffering can take our eyes off this world and ourselves.

14. Suffering can teach us firsthand that God truly is sufficient.

15. Suffering can connect us with other people.

16. Suffering can create an opportunity for witness.

17. Suffering can lead a person into Christian ministry.

18. Suffering can make us grateful for what we had or still have.

19. Suffering can position our lives to bring more glory to God.

20. Suffering, properly handled, will result in rewards in heaven.

Both the Bible and history are replete with examples of overcomers—people for whom suffering became a springboard to spiritual growth and personal accomplishments. In no way do I mean to be trite or to minimize the pain that many people have gone through, but even in the midst of a fallen, wounded, suffering world, there is ample proof that God is in the "restoration business." Consider these overcomers:

- *Demosthenes*, often called the greatest orator of the ancient world, stuttered. The first time he tried to make a public speech, he was laughed off the platform.

• *Napoleon Bonaparte* graduated from military school *forty-sixth* in a class of 65 students.

• *Ludwig van Beethoven*, one of history's greatest composers, was deaf his entire life.

• *Charles Dickens* was lame.

• *Thomas Edison*, who was deaf, tried and failed so many times at inventing the light bulb that lab assistants who once admired him began to mock him.

• *John Bunyan* spent his adult life in a prison cell, but he gave Christendom a book called *Pilgrim's Progress*, which has been continuously in print since 1678.

• *Glenn Cunningham,* before setting a world record for running the mile, was burned so severely on his body that doctors predicted he would never walk again.

• *Albert Einstein* was described by various teachers as a slow learner, retarded, uneducatable, and the like.

• *George Frederick Handel* was physically challenged, yet this composer gave the world "Messiah" and the beloved "Hallelujah Chorus."

Who knows . . . your name could be added to this remarkable list of those who refused to give in to pain and suffering and went on to accomplish extraordinary feats. Like so many others, you can join the ranks of understanding that God, even through the darkest hour of anguish, has a plan.

Summary Response

Reasons why the existence of suffering does
not negate the reality of God:

Because of what this world is and is not
Because of what humans are like
Because choices yield results
Because God has acted
Because good can come
Because the story isn't over

Ending the Search, Beginning the Journey

You don't have to be an inventor to know that there's always something else to be discovered, or an explorer to know there's always more ground that could be covered, or a researcher to know there's always another fact to be unveiled. No matter what your field, the search for data is never-ending. That's especially true in our culture of up-to-the-second newsbreaks, instant stock quotes and on-the-scene reports.

Explanation, on the other hand, isn't so automatic. In fact, finding reason behind the smallest of life's events can sometimes take a lifetime in itself. Often our searches for enlightenment can leave us feeling more discouraged than empowered.

I've been around a lot of people who are searching on both sides of the tracks. Some are purely after information. They delight in hearing the most recent poll, the latest stats or the newest discoveries. Others are in it for the why-factor. They're not as concerned about *what* came to be as much as *how* and *why*. But ultimately, everyone is on a search for something, whether they're aware of it or not.

Some people spend their entire lives searching for meaning and fulfillment. I recently read that the highest rates of suicide and divorce occur among the most affluent classes of society. On the West Coast, psychologists and counselors have isolated a new affliction and have called it "Sudden Acquired Wealth

Syndrome." People are achieving everything that our society says should make them happy, but they're finding that it's possible to be materially rich yet spiritually bankrupt. It takes more than money, fame, luxurious houses, good looks, nice cars or an impressive stock portfolio to really fill the human heart.

In my years of studying and interacting with people, I've discovered that basically our search boils down to six fundamental elements and questions that intermittently occupy our thoughts and feelings throughout life. My ministry involvement with thousands of people has helped me identify what I call the six ways we're led by head and by heart.

First, there are the three pervasive intellectual issues we ponder:

1. Origin—Where do I come from?
2. Purpose—Why am I here?
3. Destiny—Where am I going?

Then there are the three persistent emotional issues with which we grapple:

1. Acceptance—Do I fit in?
2. Significance—Do I matter?
3. Security—Am I safe?

Think about your own life. Which of these questions consumes you right now? Maybe you've finally settled into a solid job that pays well and are now able to think about investing for the future. Maybe you're still adjusting to your new school after having to transfer last year. Or maybe, despite nearing retirement age, you're just now dealing with some of the emotional scars from your childhood that you've carried your whole life.

Padding Our Boundaries

Whatever phase you're in, I'm sure you can identify with one of these areas of questioning. But let me warn you of another thing I've noticed about people (me included, of course!). Once we find a temporary solution to one of these questions, we like to use it for defensive purposes. And that's not a good thing. What do I mean by that? Put another way, as soon as we answer the question that's most consuming us, we tend to use it as a buffer against future harm.

For example, I knew a guy in college who had a reputation throughout school as being the life of the party. If Steve was around, life was fun, full of jokes and triple-dog dares, and just an all-out exciting time. Stories about "that time Steve did such-and-such" reached legendary status on campus. No matter what the situation, this guy had a way of making it memorable.

But I knew Steve better than most, which meant I got to see him even when he wasn't at his best, when he didn't bring his *A* game. Steve had doubts and frustrations just like every other college student. He was ultimately insecure not only about his future, but about his relationships with almost everyone. Somewhere along the line, his search for significance had led to the following discovery: *If I act boisterous, crazy and fun, I'll be the life of the party. And if I'm the life of the party, people will notice and like me. And that means I matter to them.*

Steve's questions of significance were constantly covered up by his façade. As a result, he could never appear down and blue because, after all, he was responsible for making everyone have a good time.

That may be a sophomoric illustration for some of you at more advanced phases of life, but you get the point. We search for answers but often use our first discovery—even if it's not the real answer/solution—as our quick fix to ward off additional pain and hurt.

Wired for the Search

God understands our grappling with significance, destiny, security or whatever else we're dealing with. He made us exactly the way we are. And yet in our fallen state, we have lack. We're missing parts—parts that only God can fix. Knowing that, it's as if God installed in each of us little clues that would lead us to Him. If we're astute enough, we'll recognize that these major life questions, these searches for things bigger than ourselves, can ultimately only lead to one place: Jesus Christ.

The only substantive, fulfilling, meaningful answer that will last and that will transcend any circumstance we go through is Jesus Christ. He is the one who pronounces the truth of God in every area of doubt we have:

1. Origin—God made you
2. Purpose—To enjoy a blessed life and eternity with your Savior
3. Destiny—A home in heaven

Those are the easy ones, the answers that anyone can gather by skimming through the Bible. They appeal strictly to the head. But God did not make us merely intellectual beings. And as a result, we're faced with a heart that struggles to find acceptance, significance and security. Thankfully, Jesus also answers each of our heart questions with His overwhelming love.

Acceptance: God Accepts You Without Condition

No one could woo a sinner like Jesus. The prostitutes, tax collectors, beggars . . . all those considered the low-lifes whom everyone shunned were in fact the ones Jesus hung out with the most. The gospel message clearly proves that it doesn't matter what your past is or how badly you've messed up, because Jesus'

love extends beyond measure. In His loving eyes, you are welcomed and accepted.

Significance: Jesus Died on a Cross out of Love for You

The truth of the cross continually blows my mind. Ponder this:
Jesus didn't just allow the nails to be put in His sacred hands and
feet; He also held it all together while He hung there. I'm not just
talking about mentally holding it together. No, Jesus—the
author of life, the sustainer of every universal law of physics—
physically kept the nails in His hands. He maintained His broken
body up on the cross, even though one word could have torn
Him off it and rightfully placed Him back on His comfortable
throne in heaven. Colossians 1:17 uses the Greek word that
means "cohesion." Christ wasn't just the crucified Savior—He
was the very glue between His suffering and our redemption.

What does this mean? It means more than life itself. Your
mom and dad may blow you off. Your stepdad may rape you.
Your wife may leave you. Your children may despise you. Your
best friend at work may stab you in the back (metaphorically
speaking) . . . but God Almighty already declared, "I will die for
you." My friend, that is proof enough that you matter to God.

Security: God Has Declared You as His

John 10:28-29 is a wonderful Scripture to keep in mind if
you're ever struggling with security issues: "And I give them
eternal life, and they shall never perish; neither shall anyone
snatch them out of My hand. My Father, who has given them
to Me, is greater than all; and no one is able to snatch them out
of My Father's hand."

Disappointments and dangers come to every life. Disasters,
such as Hurricane Katrina, can destroy your home; disease can
take away your loved one's health; death can even separate you

from your family, but the love of God makes you immovable from His grip. In Romans 8:35-39, Paul gives an extensive list of calamities that may threaten your life. But his conclusion will warm your soul:

> For I am persuaded that neither death nor life, nor angels nor principalities nor powers, nor things present nor things to come, nor height nor depth, nor any other created thing, shall be able to separate us from the love of God which is in Christ Jesus our Lord.

Back to the Basics

We've covered a lot of ground in this book. We've established the reality of God and His Word, the facts about Jesus' resurrection, and even the issues surrounding pain and suffering. But perhaps no two greater points can be made than these: 1) We are sinful; 2) God offers a remedy. Why these two? Because whether you've been a faithful Christian for 40 years or have never asked Jesus into your life, those two truths lead to the salvation that will eternally change your soul's compass.

Our condition is one of sin (see Rom. 3:23). And just as a job pays a wage at the end of a week, our sins will yield a result at the end of a lifetime. Paul lays it out clearly: "For the wages of sin is death" (Rom. 6:23). We've already discussed that the Bible describes this "death" as the ultimate worst-case scenario: eternal separation from God and the punishment of hell. Thankfully, the second half of that verse reveals the good news: "But the gift of God is eternal life in Christ Jesus our Lord." It's a gift, which means it's free. Yes, you get a free pass to eternal life with God. Now, honestly, what could be better than that?

But there's a catch. Nope, you won't be charged an extra $25 each month because you neglected to read the fine print.

The Bible is blatant about what this condition is: Jesus said, "Unless you repent you will all likewise perish" (Luke 13:3). Salvation requires repentance. What do you have to be sorry for? For your natural condition of opposition toward God. For everything you've ever done wrong. For everything you're going to do wrong. For the fact that no matter what, you'll ultimately turn against Him. Basically, you need to be sorry for your wretchedness and inadequacy (and no, those aren't to be taken lightly).

Why would God put a condition on something He wants us to say yes to? He does this because something has to be done about our sin. God, as we've already stated in this book, hates sin because of His righteousness. Yet He handled the issue by allowing His Son, Jesus Christ, to pay for the consequences of all sin for all time by giving up His life on the cross. Thankfully, we know—and have proven—the end of that story: He lives!

Because of that, you can now receive God's gift of eternal life with no strings attached. The price has been paid. All you have to do is repent from your sins and commission Jesus to become Lord of your life. Your search for meaning can end right now, and your journey to forever can begin today. It's as simple as praying something along the lines of the following prayer:

Dear Lord Jesus, I know that I've sinned and that I can't save myself. I believe that You are the Son of God, and that You died and rose again for me, to forgive my sins and to be my Savior. I turn from my sins and I ask You to forgive me. I receive You into my heart as my Lord and Savior. Jesus, thank You for saving me now. Help me to live the rest of my life for You. Amen.

As wonderful as it is to search for answers, there's nothing like finding The Answer—Jesus Christ. Trust me, after years of playing both head games and heart games, I know that He satisfies both intellectually and emotionally. He is the only sufficient answer for all time. And the reality of Jesus transcends not only time and history, but also questions and objections. He truly is the world-sized message for a heart-sized need. May you be satisfied and blessed in all your days as you journey on with Him.

"You've Decided to Believe What?!"

Instilling a Biblical Worldview in Teens Through Apologetics

The phone call came around 11:15 at night. Being a minister, this wasn't uncommon for me, but I still immediately felt a chill run through my spine and feared the worst. It was a mom and dad, upset about the changes they had seen in their son since he had been at college for a couple of years. Despite being raised in a Christian home and having been involved in church his entire life, their son had abandoned his faith. For more than an hour, these parents poured out their hearts to me.

"I'm so angry and hurt," this father confessed to me. "Four years of college have undone what we worked 18 years to instill in our son."

Their situation was especially challenging: The son was an only child, his parents' pride and joy. Although he was the valedictorian of his high school class, the young man's social skills and exposure to viewpoints other than his own had been minimal. Unprepared for university life, his heartland American innocence quickly wore off.

His first culture shock came in ethics class when he was assigned to write a paper from the viewpoint of a persecuted homosexual. When the young man spoke up in class one day against homosexuality, the professor's response humiliated him in front of his peers. Later, a class on world religions convinced him that Christianity was responsible for most of the world's problems. Meanwhile, his cultural anthropology class made him question whether or not Jesus Christ had ever existed.

The parents believed that the reason for their son's departure from the faith was because of these negative experiences that occurred to him during his college years. But spiritual skepticism was only part of the problem. Equally painful was the day their son came home on a break and, in front of several guests, broke the news that he was now gay and was living with a man in his late 50s. The parents were at their wits' end. They had a lengthy discussion with their son that night, but after things grew heated, he stormed out of the house. That's when they called me.

I have to admit, reaching out to this family was one of the most heart-wrenching experiences I've had as a minister. But what I've seen since is that it's not uncommon for young people from Christian families to experience spiritual ups and downs once they leave home. In a study involving nearly 4,000 churchgoing American teens, Josh McDowell uncovered some startling facts that should stir evangelical parents to action. What he found was that even though our teens may be in youth group or may be regular churchgoers, if they don't have a solid personal understanding of biblical truth, they will be:

- 225 percent more likely to be angry with life
- 216 percent more likely to be resentful
- 210 percent more likely to lack purpose in life
- 48 percent more likely to cheat on an exam
- 200 percent more likely to physically hurt someone
- 300 percent more likely to experiment with drugs
- 600 percent more likely to contemplate or attempt suicide[1]

The Presence and Importance of Worldview

As parents, it's vital that we take charge of our children's theological education. This starts in the classroom at school, where our sons and daughters spend the majority of their week. No, I'm not asking you to show up and sit next to your teen during biology class. What's important is that you're aware of what's being taught—and by whom.

Whether good or bad, a teacher's influence in the life of the student is deep and long lasting. Many educators provide positive influence in the lives of students. However, parents must make sure that the values taught in the home are not eroded by what's taught in the classroom. Remember that students tend to view their teachers as experts in whatever field is being taught, which gives teachers a tremendous amount of potential to shape the students' worldview. Teachers will also have the advantage of frequent personal interaction, spending hours each day with your teen.

Education extends beyond the mere communication of facts and data. The worldview held by a teacher influences all that goes on in the classroom and impacts students at a number of levels. Simply put, worldview is the way we look at reality. Author James Sire calls it "a set of assumptions (which may be true, partially true or entirely false) which you hold (consciously or subconsciously, consistently or inconsistently) about the basic makeup of the world."[2] Whether we realize it or not, we all think and live within the scope of a worldview.

The foundation and bedrock of the Christian's worldview is God and His revealed truth: God exists and may be known; He is the Creator and owner of all things and we are accountable to Him; man is made in the image of God, and human life is therefore sacred. These are but a few of the tenets comprising a believer's worldview—values that you as a Christian parent most likely have tried to impart to your children.

"I am much afraid that schools will prove to be the great gates of hell unless they diligently labor in explaining the Holy Scripture, engraving them in the hearts of youth. I advise no one to place his child where the Scriptures do not reign paramount."
—Martin Luther

Fear Not!

Just because your teen goes to a public school doesn't mean he's bound to be a brainwashed atheist. Public education doesn't necessarily conflict with a Christian education. But it's important that you realize your own role as parents in instilling a biblical perspective in *everything* your kids encounter at school. No issue is too small to hash out over dinner. No conflict is too menial that your adolescent can't call you during the middle of the day for an answer or just to vent.

Like your child's general education, instilling a solid Christian worldview isn't just about memorizing data. Discernment is a key trait that must be built. This begins with your modeling biblical discernment and truth. You can't expect your son or daughter to know right from wrong if you're not exemplifying it at home!

The key for Christian parents is to be *proactive* rather than *reactive*. Don't wait until your oldest daughter comes home from college and announces that she's now an atheist. The time to incorporate consistent biblical discipleship into your family life is now—*today*!

Don't worry, this is not as difficult as it sounds. In fact, you are probably farther along than you think. Yet wherever you are in your journey toward taking charge of your teen's theological destiny, you need to keep in mind the following points:

The Spiritual Leadership of Your Children Rests on You

In the Bible, it's a given that parents will teach God's truth to their children. From the moment your children come into your life, God's assignment to you is to nurture and grow them to the best of your ability. That includes being yielded to Him (see Josh. 24:15) as you teach them about biblical truth (see Deut. 6:7). Your views about life are to be centered on God (see Gen. 18:19) as you instill the understanding that biblical knowledge will keep your children from sin (see Ps. 119:9-11). Your children's yielding to you, their parent, is part of God's life structure (see Prov. 1:7-9; 4:1-27; 13:1).

Establish the Truth That Your Body—and Brain—Belong to God

Remember, your children—no matter how old—will pick up what you model for them. If you've always treated God as a compartment of life, guess what your kids are going to do? It's essential that you teach and exemplify a fundamental truth: You are a steward of your body and mind. Because Jesus purchased your soul and your salvation, you (thankfully) belong to Him (see 1 Cor. 6:20). That means it does matter what you put into your head, what you listen to and what you watch with your eyes. God's ownership extends to every area of your life. Teach your teens how they can yield their intellects to God (see Matt. 22:37; 2 Cor. 10:4-5; Eph. 4:17-24; 2 Tim. 3:14-17).

Always Ask God for Help

Maybe you haven't always modeled consistent Christian behavior for your family. In setting goals for family spiritual growth, you may wonder if your teens will take you seriously. These apprehensions are understandable. The Bible promises much to believers in such situations. Need wisdom? God says He will give it abundantly (see Jas. 1:5). Need a specific answer for a specific prayer? God says to ask (see Jas. 4:2). God further promises to provide for *every* real need that you have (see Phil. 4:19). And never forget that as you ask God for guidance through this journey, you can trust in His promise that He will complete His plans not just for you but also for your entire family (see Phil. 1:6).

"Oh fathers and mothers, the ruin of your children, or their salvation, will, under God, very much depend on you."
—*Charles H. Spurgeon*

Don't Procrastinate, Because Time Won't Wait for You

Don't approach life like the person who once said, "One good thing about procrastination is that you always have something planned for tomorrow!" The teen years go flying by, as I'm sure all parents of adolescents know. It's urgent that you do as much as you can to help your teen learn and live apologetics. Guide them not just toward beliefs but also toward *knowing* why they believe those things.

A Biblically Literate Family Doesn't Happen by Accident

Don't expect your teens to understand the profundities of Scripture right away. Your teens will grow up understanding what they believe and why only if *you* make a conscious decision to make your home a place of Christian education.

Growing up in the South, I was fortunate enough to often hear adults repeating bits of wisdom that had been passed down through the generations. One of my favorite that I'd hear the old-timers use was, "Chase two rabbits and they'll both escape."

In other words, be *focused*. Go after one thing a time. It's no different in setting up spiritual disciplines in your household. Here are some tips to help you follow through with this:

- Set a daily time to pray with your teens—and stick to it.

- Begin your family's own Bible literacy program. Christian bookstores have plenty of Read-the-Bible-in-a-Year choices. You'll be amazed at how quickly daily Bible reading can become a natural part of your day. There is great benefit in reading the Bible through in its entirety.

- Read the Gospel of John through in one month (with only 21 chapters, this can be done in only minutes per day).

- Read through the Bible's book of wisdom (Proverbs, only 31 chapters) in one month.

- Talk with your teens about their spiritual life. What are their areas of doubt or struggle? What issues in the Bible do they have a hard time grasping? Let them know that they can talk with you about *anything*. The important thing is to keep a steady dialogue going.

- Practice sharing your salvation testimony with your teens. Talk about your life before your met Christ, how you met Christ, and how He's changed your life. Establish the importance of sharing your faith with others by doing exactly that in your own life. Let your teen know that your family is not ashamed of the gospel (see Rom. 1:16).

- Work on Scripture memory together. Heed the Bible's call to hide God's Word in your heart (see Ps. 119:11). Learning one verse per month is a realistic goal. Practice reciting memory verses and quizzing each other.

- Exercise discernment in both the content and quantity of media that you allow into your home. Make entertainment choices that are appropriate for a Christian family. Set boundaries and stick to them. Help your teen understand *why* it's important for Christians to guard their hearts (see Prov. 4:23; Ps. 101:2-3).

- Encourage your teen to read good books on the Bible and about apologetics. Build a resource library for your family, making sure that your teen is informed on the key apologetics topics (such as the ones addressed in this book).

Set Your Priorities

If you're serious about your family building their lives on biblical truths, you can't just treat it as another phase you're in. Teaching your teens about faith must be a top priority, or else it becomes yet another thing to let slide. Many Christian parents are paying the price for not teaching the truth of God's Word to their teens. It's time to allow biblical truths and apologetics change decades-old trends. Take time with your teens on a regular basis to teach, explain, impart and mold. Consider these years as an investment that will count for eternity.

Become Convicted

No, I'm not saying that you should go to jail. I'm saying that you should become passionate and be single-minded as you head toward the goal of seeing your kids firmly rooted in their faith.

Did you ever hear about the man who said about himself, "I used to think I was indecisive, but now I'm not too sure"? I've found that the families who enjoy spiritual stability are those that are founded on *convictions*. Convictions include principles, truths, beliefs, parameters and boundaries that are known, understood and accepted by everyone in the family. The convictions of a family are bigger than feelings, are unshaken by circumstances, and should be informed by the parent's knowledge of God's Word.

Don't Lose the Battle for Your Teens

To lead your family in God's *ways*, you must be committed to God's *Word*. Remember that personal Christian growth and the effective teaching of teens have little to do with *feelings*. Building a Christian family (with God's help, of course) is an act of *will*. Determine right now that above all else, your family will be grounded in God's Word.

I once heard a Christian husband say that he and his wife adopted this motto for their home: *"We may lose at everything else, but we will win with our children."* In the area of grooming the minds of our teens, sadly, many evangelical parents have already lost the battle. My prayer—and my purpose in writing this book—is that in this age of unrelenting darkness, individuals will go the distance for Christ.

For the sake of future Christian generations, make Jesus the Lord of your life. Make Him the leader of your home. View your family interactions as an offering of worship to the Lord and live out your relationships with your teens as authentically, genuinely and consistently as you can.

I honestly believe that Jesus does not expect great, one-time heroics from us. The Lord blesses (and works through) basic day-to-day fidelity, faithfulness and simple obedience.

A 12-Week Apologetics Study Guide

For Small Groups and Sunday School Classes

Although the majority of my time is spent speaking in front of congregations and large assemblies of people, I'm a big fan of small groups. Most often, that's the atmosphere that breeds in-depth discussion, heart-to-heart dialogue and life-changing revelation.

This book was written with exactly that in mind. And it's why I've included this 12-week guide for small groups wanting to use *The 10 Most Common Objections to Christianity* as a study resource. Don't feel obligated to only do this at a church, however. Hopefully, you'll agree that this book doesn't toss around a bunch of indecipherable Christianese or churchy lingo. As stated early on, I've kept in mind that many nonbelievers, skeptics and cynics may pick up this book out of curiosity—you know, just to check out what "those guys" are saying. As such, don't assume that everyone coming to your group sessions will be Christian.

In your preparations for this 12-week study, allow me to mention a few things to consider as you lead the group.

1. Make It Fun

The word "apologetics" is already intimidating enough to some people. It's important that you create a relaxed atmosphere that's conducive to learning but also enjoyable. This isn't a brainiacs meeting, so make sure people of any intellectual level feel welcomed.

2. Keep It Timely

One of the greatest things about apologetics is that it's applicable on an everyday basis. Throughout the week, keep watch for TV shows, movies, events, articles and news reports that tie in with your study. Bring clips of them to stir up discussion. Ask group members for their opinions on these events. Faith is a hot issue right now in the secular world, and the media loves to cover the hot-button topics, so there will be no shortage of relevant outside material.

3. Stay on Target

Without fail, talking about topics such as the existence of God, creationism and the issue of pain stirs up conversation. But with that, it's easy for groups to get sidetracked by secondary issues. That doesn't mean you, as the leader, don't have the freedom to allow conversation to flow naturally and take its own course. But as a guide, your responsibility is to maintain the group's purpose for the week. As the study progresses, you'll get a feel for how authoritative you have to be. Usually, it's a less-is-better rule, but sometimes commanding leadership is essential for the benefit of all.

Some Practical Considerations
Do . . .

- Have everyone read the chapter before each week's meeting.
- Begin each session with prayer.
- Have yourself (or some other Christian) moderate the

discussion, and appropriately bring closure to each session.

- Pray for the Holy Spirit to control the sessions.
- Offer to talk further with anyone who has spiritual needs.
- Compare and contrast how Christianity and other belief systems differ.
- Encourage open discussion.
- Admit when you don't know the answer to something.
- Let the group members know that you genuinely care about them.
- Keep Jesus Christ as the focal point.

Don't . . .

- Act like you know it all.
- Make anyone feel like he or she has asked a dumb question.
- Dumb down the discussions.
- Freak out at unexpected comments or emotions.
- Raise more questions than you answer.
- Leave without bringing appropriate closure to a question or issue.
- Publicly criticize or attack specific Christian denominations or individuals.

With that in mind, have fun. Cover yourself in prayer and always, *always* ask the Holy Spirit to guide your every direction and word as you lead the group. Go forth and discover why you believe what you believe!

Introduction
The Questions of Life

First five minutes: Welcome/begin with prayer.
Read: Psalm 119:30; Isaiah 59:14-15
Ask:

1. How do *you* determine what's true? How does our culture define truth?
2. Is truth always absolute? What does the Bible say is truth? (See Mal. 3:6; Pss. 25:10; 89:14; 90:2; 117:2; 119:142,151,160; Heb. 13:8.)
3. Whether or not you're a Christian, in what ways have you encountered opposition toward your personal beliefs?
4. What's your motive for reading this book? What are your expectations?
5. Should apologetics be required learning for every believer? Why or why not?

Summary

"That's true for you, but not for me. Truth means different things to different people . . . there's no one absolute truth for everybody."

Ever had your Christian perspective rebutted by statements like this? You may not walk around thinking about the nature of truth nor may you routinely use words such as "epistemology," but Christians today have the important job of presenting and explaining truth within a culture that's sure you *can't* be sure.

The Bible teaches that truth is related to the character of God, which means it is eternal and unchanging. It doesn't have an expiration date, nor does it ever go out of style (despite how our culture today treats it). The problem is, not everyone accepts the Bible as the ultimate authority. Some don't even subscribe to the "notion" that God exists. We'll tackle both those issues in future weeks. Before we get there, however, it's essential to know that whenever you talk to someone about the foundations of your faith, truth must be established as an absolute.

That's where apologetics comes in. Apologetics is the ultimate combination of faith and reason. It's the defense for what you believe. (Sadly, in some relativistic circles, it's become the last line of defense for God.) It's the "why" behind every heartbeat. But thankfully, for every true believer, it's further cause to worship the ultimate Truth, Jesus Christ.

Objection No. 1:
God Is Not Real

First five minutes: Welcome/begin with prayer.
Read: Romans 1:19-21; Hebrews 11:6
Ask:

1. Have you ever doubted God's existence? If you believe in God, what first caused you to believe in Him?
2. What are some reasons people have for not believing in God's existence?
3. In your own words, explain how those arguments stack up against what you've learned in this chapter.
4. Do you agree that it takes more faith to be an atheist or agnostic than it does to believe in God? Why or why not?
5. What proof of God's existence most resonates in your life?

Summary

In Psalm 14:1, we read, "The fool says in his heart, 'There is no God.' They are corrupt, their deeds are vile; there is no one who does good" (*NIV*). The word rendered "fool" in this verse (and in other Psalms) is a Hebrew term denoting "one who is morally deficient." In the politically correct climate in which we live, it's certainly not popular to point out that atheism is a moral as well as spiritual issue. But the words of Scripture, chosen by the Holy Spirit, bear this out.

We can't help but look to a supernatural source to explain certain patterns and exceptions in life—a universal sense of good and evil, moral knowledge, nature's rhythms, and so forth. Thankfully, as believers we can do more than just point to or acknowledge this God; we can know Him. He is personal by His very nature.

Obviously, people have a variety of reasons for not believing in God. Yet all of them, as we've seen in this chapter, amount to little. Next week, we'll see how they amount to *nothing* in light of the universe around us.

Objection No. 2:
Creation Is a Myth

First five minutes: Welcome/begin with prayer.
Read: Genesis 1:1-2:7; Psalm 19:1-4
Ask:

1. Whether you believe in creation or evolution, how does the Bible's account of the origin of life reflect what we know about the universe?
2. How has the term "evolution" been watered down to become more acceptable even among Christians?

3. What parts of the creationism argument are irrefutable?
4. Is intelligent design just a cop-out? How does it differ from creationism? Why is it causing such a stir in the science and academia communities?
5. How could talk about science and creation prompt you to worship?

Summary

The creation vs. evolution debate may go down in history as the twentieth and twenty-first centuries' most heated topic in certain circles. But it also could go down in history as humanity's most arrogant moment: A creation defying its creator. Who would have thought? And yet isn't that the core of sin? In our ultimate rebellion, we've claimed man-made science to rule over a sovereign God.

So how does God respond? Psalm 94:9 says, "He who planted the ear, shall He not hear? He who formed the eye, shall He not see?" In other words, God says, "Do you not think I notice what's going on?" God sees our debate. He's watching every evolutionist shake his "ape-evolved" fist toward the sky in challenge to Him. It's safe for us to say that the God of the universe, the Creator of all life, is certainly up for the challenge. And at some point, He will have had enough. At some point in history, the rants of godless humans will finally—thank God—be silenced.

Objection No. 3:
The Bible Is Not Completely Authentic

First five minutes: Welcome/begin with prayer.
Read: Psalms 33:4; 119:18,160
Ask:

1. How has our society suffered by not honoring—much less believing—the Bible as God's Word?
2. In what ways do most people combine the accuracy and the authenticity of the Bible in their opinion of it? Is that fair?
3. What are the two factors involved in evaluating the authenticity of an ancient manuscript? How does the Bible measure up to other texts?
4. Why do you think the Word's validity is so debated despite the resounding evidence proving its legitimacy?
5. Biblical conspiracies and pop-culture myths seem to emerge with every new generation. What role does apologetics play in combating these?

Summary

The facts are overwhelming: *thousands* of manuscript copies, compared to the mere dozens for other unquestioned texts; a minimal amount of time between the events and the writings. And yet the Bible is still scrutinized as a historical document. For the Christian, it's imperative to be able to point to these facts simply because our morals—our entire system of truth—are based on God's Word being real. Too often believers take for granted the overwhelming data that proves the Bible isn't some hoax, and yet we stand by while doubters mock its validity with paper-thin claims.

There is no greater document than the Bible. That truth stands on multiple levels. But perhaps none is more important than how your spirit soars with its words. This week, ask God to show you His Word's powers. Ask Him to bring it to life for you. And be amazed at the masterful strokes of the Holy Spirit behind this timeless, impenetrable classic.

Objection No. 4:
The Bible Is Not Completely Accurate

First five minutes: Welcome/begin with prayer.
Read: 2 Timothy 4:3-4; Psalm 119:160
Ask:

1. What are some of the errors you've heard the Bible contains? (Leader, be prepared for some silence here!)
2. Why do we assume that antiquity automatically implies error? Are there other old books that have been proven wrong with age?
3. What would you say to someone who claims the Bible can mean different things to different people?
4. Picture yourself as a writer of one of the Bible's books. What reaction do you think you would have received back then if you claimed to be writing the divine words of God Himself? How were these writers' claims substantiated?
5. How do you think God intended His Word to be received: literally without exception? figuratively without exception? a mixture of the two? (And if it's a blend, how do we decide which parts are literal and which are figurative?)

Summary

Isn't it amazing how people still argue over the Bible's so-called "mistakes"? They automatically assume that since the Bible is so old, it *has to* contain errors. Yet the Word is astounding in its inerrancy. Even modern-day transcriptions of popular books go awry through updated versions and revisions. And yet God's Word—in every case throughout thousands of years—has been perfectly preserved.

As Jesus said, "Not the smallest letter, not the least stroke of a pen, will by any means disappear from the Law until everything is accomplished" (Matt. 5:18, *NIV*). Christ wasn't speaking figuratively there; He was being quite literal. The Old Testament, written in Hebrew, contained millions of jots and tittles that were intrinsic to the language. Yet not one stroke, not even a single comma, has been changed in the Bible.

For Christians, this isn't just a matter of the Bible's strength as a literary book. It's an astounding, humbling sign of God's power. His Word truly will last forever!

Objection No. 5:
Jesus Was Just a Man

First five minutes: Welcome/begin with prayer.
Read: John 7:46; 8:58; 1 Corinthians 15:14-20
Ask:

1. Name some of the labels that are applied to Jesus.
2. How was Jesus unique?
3. Strictly in terms of apologetics, why is the resurrection the crux of history?
4. Why have so many lawyers and legal minds been persuaded by the case for Christ?
5. How do we know that Jesus came back from the dead?

Summary

Without Jesus, without His crucifixion and resurrection, Christianity would be an incomplete religion. Can you imagine if Jesus had never come to Earth? Most likely, true believers—God-honoring believers—would be a dime a dozen. And yet all because of Jesus' sacrifice, the doors have been flung wide open. God's mercy, grace, forgiveness and love have been offered freely. And yet look how the world responds: *Jesus wasn't real. Jesus was just a great teacher. Jesus was a psychotic case with some good points to make.*

Perhaps no chapter in this book is as crucial as this one when it comes to understanding what you face as a Christian. The world doesn't want to believe. It doesn't want to believe in God. It doesn't want to acknowledge the Bible. And it certainly doesn't want to admit that Jesus is God's Son.

But the facts are there. The evidence speaks for itself. Christ came, died and conquered. He was the real deal. As Christ-followers, let's know how to defend His truth by the world's standards—with facts. And yet in the process, may we always remember that our Savior put aside the head games and condensed His truth to one question: Who do you say I am?

Objection No. 6:
Jesus Is Not the Only Way to Heaven

First five minutes: Welcome/begin with prayer.
Read: John 14:6; Acts 4:12
Ask:

1. What comments have you heard from others when talking about heaven? How do they describe it? What are their credentials for getting in?

2. Why does the world abhor the idea that Jesus is the only way to heaven?

3. How can a Christian respond to the accusation of being narrow-minded and intolerant?

4. Why do you think God made His kingdom so "exclusive" and yet so available?

5. What does the Bible say about Judaism, Islam and any other religion that claims to worship God?

Summary

It's not easy to live shoulder to shoulder in a relativistic society with people of other faiths and claim that yours is the only true way to an afterlife. And yet that's exactly what Christians inherently do by claiming Jesus Christ as Lord. So why can't there possibly be more ways to God? Why do we have to be so exclusive?

Two reasons: (1) God defines the rules of heaven, not us. It's His kingdom we're after. Most of us already accept the fact that if this world is all we're living for, we might as well check out now. And (2) Jesus has every right to be restrictive with His requirements. He's the only person in history who's entered the realm of death and come back to speak of it under His own power. That wasn't just a one-time feat. Jesus earned the praises of all heaven and Earth for all eternity. And to enter into that eternity, He makes the simple request to acknowledge Him for who He's already proven He is. Now, think of it from a logistical standpoint: How "narrow-minded" is that?

Objection No. 7:
A Loving God Wouldn't Send People to Hell

First five minutes: Welcome/begin with prayer.
Read: Genesis 6:3; 2 Peter 3:9
Ask:

1. When do you feel like you've experienced hell on Earth? After reading this chapter, do you still feel like your experience was a literal piece of hell?
2. Why do you think hell seems unreal for some people?
3. When and how do you think hell began? What does the Bible say about this?
4. Why is the punishment part of hell necessary? Why couldn't God just have disallowed those people into heaven, as opposed to making them suffer?
5. Explain the "Africa question." How would you answer this so-called quandary in your own words?

Summary

Only when we get a *real* glimpse of hell, of its unspeakably horrific reality, can the urgency of the gospel settle on us. Jesus understood this while on Earth. He knew that hell was necessary because of our sinfulness and God's righteousness. And He also knew He would have to face hell to provide us with a way to avoid it. Otherwise, it would be the final destination for every soul who ever lived—no ifs, ands or buts. Yet by His sacrifice, by His powerful victory, we now have the amazing opportunity to change that doomed destiny.

With this in mind, Christians *must*—I can't emphasize that more—have a sense of urgency for evangelizing. We must show people the light of Jesus so that they can know His name, acknowledge Him as the true Savior, and turn from the flames of hell. In a way, that's what this study is all about. Explaining the reasons behind certain theological beliefs is good, but pointing a soul in the right direction must be the ultimate goal. By your simple yet profound, reasoned assurance of faith, you can lead others on a path toward an eternity with God. Don't lose sight of that fact in these final weeks!

<hr>

Objection No. 8:
People Are Basically Good

First five minutes: Welcome/begin with prayer.
Read: Psalms 66:18; 139:23-24
Ask:

1. The first verse we read says God would not have listened if the psalmist had "cherished sin in my heart" (*NIV*). Why would he say something like this? Does God really not listen to us when we harbor sin? Why is it necessary to acknowledge our sinfulness in order for Him to move in our lives?
2. What consequences of sin have you seen today?
3. How are we often unaware of our sin?
4. Why do we rank sins? Where do you think that originated?
5. How have you tried to compensate for your sinfulness? What "works" have you tried to put on your spiritual résumé to impress God?

Summary
Really now, is human sin *that* serious? Does it really matter that much when we tell a little white lie every now and then, or when

we fudge on our taxes just a little? Consider the facts laid out in Isaiah 53:5: "But He was pierced for our transgressions, He was crushed for our iniquities; the punishment that brought us peace was upon Him, and by His wounds we are healed" (*NIV*). That's talking about Jesus. More specifically, that's talking about what our sin—yes even one "little" one—did to Him.

Many people today refuse to talk about sin. Some say it's negative and bad for self-esteem. Others—Christians—say that it's a non-issue since Jesus paid for it all. And while they're right about Jesus' redeeming work on the cross, sin is still an issue for us because we live in a sinful, fallen world. We're wading through the consequences of our own state.

That's why the good news is exactly that to those who believe. Through Jesus' payment, we have been declared clean for life. Do we still sin? You bet. But it no longer has the consequences of death attached to it. That's reason to worship. Better yet, that's reason, as Jesus told one sinner in the Bible, to "go and sin no more" (John 8:11).

Objection No. 9:
Christians Are All Hypocrites

First five minutes: Welcome/begin with prayer.
Read: Romans 8:19-22; John 16:33
Ask:

1. Before you became a Christian, or even if you're not a Christian now, what turned/turns you off the most about following God?
2. The Crusades and the Inquisition were major blunders in Christian history. What other less-glaring

times can you think of in which the Church at large
has appeared hypocritical?

3. What can you do to overcome the perception that
   all Christians are hypocrites?

4. Do you feel Christians are judged more harshly than
   people of other religions? Why or why not?

5. Obviously, Christians are targets (of the media, of culture, of intellectual skeptics) when it comes to being
   "caught on tape" with a screw-up. What's the best
   response to both your Christian and non-Christian
   friends when someone else's sin is exposed?

Summary

"If any one of you is without sin, let him be the first to throw a stone at her."

Those are the infamous words of Jesus to a crowd of trigger-
happy scribes and Pharisees about to stone a woman caught having sex outside of marriage (see John 8:1-12, *NIV*). Even though
this took place 2,000 years ago, the scene could just as well have
been from today. We're all so ready to condemn others. For many
non-Christians, their primary reason for not trusting God with
their life is simply because they're turned off by believers not acting completely holy 100 percent of the time. And even among
Christians, we often hold up a radar gun to search out for yet
another perpetrator to offend us beyond apology.

The truth is, we all stink. We're all covered in the grimy filth
of sinfulness by nature. The only difference is that Christians at
least have an assurance that they've been cleansed. But for us
believers, we've got to stop pointing fingers, or we'll wind up in
the same place as the Pharisees—with Jesus offering us a big fat
"woe to you."

We learned last week—as if it were anything new—that we're
all sinners. That puts us all in the same boat. For those who have
been saved, it's only because of Jesus. And for those who will be

saved, it's all because of Jesus. Get the point? As Christ said after saving the adulterous woman and forgiving her sins, "I am the light of the world. He who follows Me shall not walk in darkness, but have the light of life." Let's cast aside the bad rap, the regretful moments and the generalizations of Christianity and concentrate on exposing that light to those around us.

Objection No. 10:
A Merciful God Wouldn't Allow Suffering

First five minutes: Welcome/begin with prayer.
Read: Romans 8:18-22; John 16:33
Ask:

1. When have you blamed God for something that went wrong in your life?
2. Does God ever cause suffering, or does He just allow it? Is there a difference?
3. Name some situations where you have watched a seemingly innocent person suffer. What thoughts or questions has it roused in you? Do you have answers?
4. How can you process troubles so that they bring you closer to God rather than drive you away from God?
5. In your life, how has God used pain as a "megaphone"?

Summary
When author Robert Louis Stevenson was near the end of his life, he became extremely ill. He continued writing until his fingers curled up and he could no longer hold a pen. When that happened, he dictated to a secretary until his voice became so

hoarse that he no longer had the strength to speak for long periods of time. Yet through his increasing illness, he maintained a positive attitude.

As his wife came in each morning, Stevenson would look up from his bed and give her a big smile. One morning, his wife spoke out sarcastically, saying, "Wait—before you speak, I suppose you are going to say, 'Isn't this a beautiful day that God has given us?'"

Stevenson paused and said, "As a matter of fact, yes, that is exactly what I was about to say. I do not intend to let a row of medicine bottles on a shelf become the extent of my horizon."

Pain is a two-way street. It can drive us away from or toward God. No matter if it's a stubbed toe or a lost child, it's our choice as to how we react. As you delve deeper into the reasons why you believe that God does not cause suffering and why evil exists in the world, keep this in mind: It's a challenging thing to watch a baby die and say that God is good. And yet He is. If you're still struggling deep inside with this, ask Him this week to unveil more of His goodness, more of His transforming truth, in your life.

Conclusion
Ending the Search, Beginning the Journey

First five minutes: Welcome/begin with prayer.
Read: Matthew 7:7; John 14:6; Philippians 3:12-14
Ask:

1. Which of the six head and heart issues do you wrestle with the most on a consistent basis? How have you answered the questions that come from that struggle?

2. In all honesty, do you feel accepted, significant and secure? Do you have a sense of origin, purpose and destiny? Explain.

3. *Sacrifice. Justice. Forgiveness. Heroism. Hope. Inspiration. Love.* What feelings do these words stir within you? How do each of these relate to what Jesus did through the cross and resurrection?
4. Where would you say you are on your journey with God? Where are you on your search for truth?
5. How has this book helped you in regards to understanding why you believe what you believe?

Summary

If you're like most people who've been through what this book is all about, you're experiencing several emotions right now. Relief. Pride. Excitement. Encouragement. Maybe you're even feeling a little overwhelmed. Hopefully, you're inspired to delve deeper into your faith than ever before. Just because you've gotten through the 10 most common objections doesn't mean there aren't more questions that will come flying in your face from the staunchest of doubters. People—especially skeptics—ask good, tough questions. And as Christians, it's our calling to be prepared.

Keep in mind what's been the motto of my own life: "But sanctify the Lord God in your hearts, and always be ready to give a defense to everyone who asks you a reason for the hope that is in you" (1 Pet. 3:15).

But most of all, let's never forget that as wonderful as apologetics is, as great as it is to unfold the reason and understanding behind your faith, as excellent as it is to prepare yourself wholeheartedly for the doubters and skeptics in the world, and as honorable as it is to desire to defend the faith, our purpose on Earth isn't to fill our heads with more knowledge. Our purpose is to worship and glorify the reason behind our faith. May you honor Jesus above all as you continue your journey with Him.

ENDNOTES

Introduction: The Questions of Life

1. Jerry Adler, "In Search of the Spiritual," *Newsweek* (August 29, 2005), p. 46.
2. *Newsweek*/Beliefnet national poll of 1,004 adults, www.belief net.com.
3. Josh McDowell and Bob Hostetler, *The New Tolerance*, (Wheaton, IL: Tyndale Publishers, 1998), p. 174.
4. Ron Bond and Peter B. Smith, "Culture and Conformity: A Meta-Analysis of Studies Using Asch's Line Judgement Task," *Psychological Bulletin*, vol. 119, no. 1, pp. 111-137.
5. R. C. Sproul, *Now That's a Good Question!* (Wheaton, IL: Tyndale Publishers, 1996), p. 14.
6. W. E. Vine, *Vine's Expository Dictionary of New Testament Word* (Nashville, TN: Thomas Nelson, 1940), p. 53.
7. Ibid, pp. 924-925.
8. "Public Arts Culture News and Reviews," *All Things Considered*, National Public Radio.

Objection No. 1: God Is Not Real

1. Tom Carter, ed., *2,200 Quotations from the Writings of Charles H. Spurgeon* (Grand Rapids, MI: Baker Books, 1988), p. 16.
2. Carl Sagan, *Cosmos* (New York: Ballantine Books, 1985), pp. 1-2.
3. Carter, *2,200 Quotations from the Writings of Charles H. Spurgeon*, p. 12.
4. *Contact*, Warner Brothers USA, 1997.
5. J. Budziszewski, *Written on the Heart: The Case for Natural Law* (Downers Grove, IL: Intervarsity Press, 1997), pp. 208-209.
6. C. S. Lewis, *The Abolition of Man* (New York: MacMillan Books, 1947), p. 41.

7. Ibid.

8. Quoted by Damon Linker in "Nietzsche's Truth," *First Things,* August/September 2002, pp. 50-60.

9. Quoted in "Anythingbuttery," *To the Source,* September 20, 2005. http://www.tothesource.org.

10. J. P. Moreland, *Scaling the Secular City* (Grand Rapids, MI: Baker Books, 1987), p. 18.

Objection No. 2: Creation Is a Myth

1. Nancy Pearcy, "We're Not in Kansas Anymore," *Christianity Today* (May 22, 2000), pp. 43-49.

2. Francis Darwin, ed., *Charles Darwin Life and Letters, Vol. 1.*, p. 285.

3. Peter Slevin, "Teachers, Scientists Vow to Fight Challenge to Evolution," *The Washington Post* (May 5, 2005), p. 3.

4. Associated Press, "University Adds Class on 'Mythology' of Creationism," *Colorado Springs Gazette* (November 21, 2005), A11.

5. Rick Wiess, "Many Scientists Admit Misconduct," *Washington Post* (June 9, 2005), A3.

6. Ibid.

7. Associated Press, "Stem Cell Work Faked, School Says," *Colorado Springs Gazette* (December 23, 2005).

8. Lawrence M. Krauss, "The End of the Age Problem and the Case for a Cosmological Constant Revisited," *Astrophysical Journal* (1998), pp. 461-466.

9. Gregg Easterbrook, "The New Convergence," *Wired* (December 2002). http://www.wired.com/wired/archive/10.12/convergence.html?pg=2&topic=&topic_set= (accessed December 2006).

10. Charles Seife, *Alpha and Omega* (New York: Viking Penguin, 2003), pp. 187-188.

11. Fred Hoyle and N. Chandra Wickramasinghe, *Evolution from Space: A Theory of Cosmic Creationism* (New York: Simon and Schuster, 1981), p. 141.

12. Geoffrey Simmons, *What Darwin Didn't Know* (Eugene, OR: Harvest House, 2004), p. 38.

13. Richard Dawkins, *The Blind Watchmaker* (New York: W. W. Norton, 1987), p. 229.

14. Duane Schmidt, *And God Created Darwin: The Death of Darwinian Evolution* (Fairfax, VA: Allegiance Press, 2001).

15. Simmons, *What Darwin Didn't Know*, pp. 305-306.

16. Jill Lawless, "Typing Monkeys Don't Write Shakespeare," Associated Press (May 9, 2003).

17. "William Dembski on Intelligent Design," *The Colorado Contender* (April 2005).

18. Michael Lemonick, "How Man Began," *Time* magazine (March 14, 1999).

19. Leslie E. Orgel, "The Origin of Life on the Earth," *Scientific American* (October 1994), p. 78.

20. Jeffrey Schwartz, *Sudden Origins* (New York: John Wiley, 1999), p. 300.

21. N. A. Takahata, "Genetic Perspective on the Origin and History of Humans," *Annual Review of Ecology and Systematics* (Vol. 26, 1995).

22. Ralph Muncaster, *How to Talk About Jesus with the Skeptics in Your Life* (Eugene, OR: Harvest House Publishers, 2001), p. 33.

23. Strobel, *The Case for a Creator*, p. 230.

24. Quoted in "The Language of Our Cells," *Y-Origins* (Orlando, FL: B & L Publications, 2004), p. 56.

25. Richard Dawkins, "Put Your Money on Evolution," quoted in Maitland A. Edey and Donald C. Johanson, "Blueprints: Solving the Mystery of Evolution," *New York Times* (April 9, 1989), sec. 7, p. 34.

26. Tanner Edis, "Darwin in Mind: Intelligent Design Meets Artificial Intelligence," *Skeptical Enquirer* (March/April 2001), pp. 35-39.

27. George Greenstein, *The Symbiotic Universe* (New York: William Morrow, 1988), p. 27.

Objection No. 3: The Bible Is Not Completely Authentic

1. Stephen L. Carter, "Liberalism's Religion Problem," *First Things* (March 2002), pp. 21-32.

2. Josh McDowell and Don Stewart, *Answers to Tough Questions Skeptics Ask About the Christian Faith,* (San Bernardino, CA: Here's Life Publishers, 1980), p. 1.

3. Norman Geisler, *Systematic Theology, Volume 1* (Minneapolis, MN: Bethany House, 2002), p. 439.

4. "Towards a More Conservative View," *Christianity Today* (January 18, 1963).

5. Windfried Corduan, *No Doubt About It* (Nashville, TN: Broadman & Holman, 1997), p. 193.

6. Frederick Kenyon, *Our Bible and the Ancient Manuscripts, 4ᵗʰ edition* (New York: Harper & Row, 1958), p. 55.

7. F. F. Bruce, *The New Testament Documents: Are They Reliable?* rev. ed. (Grand Rapids, MI: William B. Eerdmans Publishing Co., 1977), p. 15.

8. Gary R. Habermas, *The Historical Jesus: Ancient Evidence for the Life of Christ* (Joplin, MI: College Press, 1996), p. 154.

9. Ibid., p. 98. Originally found in Louis Cassels, "Debunkers of Jesus Still Trying," *The Detroit News* (June 23, 1973), 7A.

10. Ben Lynfield, "New Find, Old Tomb, and Peeks at Early Christians," *Christian Science Monitor* (December 18, 2003).

11. Karin Laub, "Scholars Discover New Testament Inscription," Associated Press (November 21, 2003).

12. Norman Geisler, *Baker Encyclopedia of Christian Apologetics* (Grand Rapids, MI: Baker Books, 1999), p. 614.

13. Peter W. Stoner and Robert C. Newman, *Science Speaks* (Chicago, IL: Moody Press, 1976).

14. Nelson Gluek, *Rivers in the Desert: A History of the Negev* (New York: Farar, Strauss & Cudahy, 1959), p. 136.

Objection No. 4: The Bible Is Not Completely Accurate

1. Wilbur M. Smith, *The Supernaturalness of Christ* (Boston, MA: W. A. Wilde Company, 1954), p. 205.

2. Ken Ham, *Where Did Cain Get His Wife?* (Florence, KY: Answers In Genesis, 1997), p. 1.

3. Norman Geisler and Thomas Howe, *When Critics Ask* (Grand Rapids, MI: Baker Books, 1997), pp. 384-385.

4. Dorothy Sayers, *The Man Born to Be King: A Play-Cycle on the Life of Our Lord and Savior Jesus Christ* (New York: Harper & Brothers, 1943), p. 19.

Objection No. 5: Jesus Was Just a Man

1. Thomas Arnold, *Sermons on Christian Life, Its Fears and Its Close*, 6th ed. (London: n.p., 1854), p. 324.

2. James Strong, *A Greek Dictionary of the New Testament* (Grand Rapids, MI: Baker Book House, 1981), p. 71.

3. Michael Green, *Man Alive* (Downers Grove, IL: InterVarsity Press, 1968), pp. 53-54.

4. Simon Greenleaf, *An Examination of the Testimony of the Four Evangelists by the Rules of Evidence* (Grand Rapids, MI: Baker Book House, 1965).

5. Lee Strobel, *The Case for Christ* (Grand Rapids, MI: Zondervan Publishing House, 1998), p. 201.

6. Gerd Ludemann, *The Resurrection of Christ: A Historical Inquiry* (Amherst, NY: Promethius, 2004), p. 50.

7. Quoted by John R. Stott, *Basic Christianity* (London: Intervarsity, 1969), p. 47.

8. Gary R. Habermas, *The Historical Jesus: Ancient Evidence for the Life of Christ* (Joplin, MO: College Press Publishing Company, 1996), pp. 146–152.

9. J. N. D. Anderson, *Christianity: The Witness of History* (London: Tyndale Press, 1970), p. 105.

10. Gary R. Habermas and Michael Licona, *The Case for the*

Resurrection of Jesus (Grand Rapids, MI: Kregel Publications, 2004), p. 52.

11. List compiled by Gary Habermas, *The Historical Jesus: Ancient Evidence for the Life of Christ*, pp. 146–152.

12. C. S. Lewis, *Mere Christianity* (New York: Macmillan Publishing Co., 1975), pp. 55-56.

13. Bertrand Russell, *Why I Am Not a Christian* (New York: Simon and Schuster, 1957), p. 16.

14. Quoted in Larry Chapman, ed., "Born Identity," *Y-Jesus: Who Was the Real Jesus*, vol. 2 (Orlando, FL: B&L Publications, 2005), p. 7.

15. Josh McDowell, *Evidence That Demands a Verdict*, vol. 1 (Nashville, TN: Thomas Nelson, 1979), p. 87.

16. Will Durant, "Caesar and Christ," *The Story of Civilization*, vol. 3. (New York: Simon & Schuster, 1972), pp. 73, 281.

17. Chapman, "Born Identity," p. 12.

18. Habermas, *The Case for the Resurrection of Jesus*, pp. 266-270, 284-285.

19. Reuters, "Did Jesus Exist? Court to Decide" (January 4, 2006).

20. Strobel, *The Case for Christ*, pp. 81, 86.

21. Michael Grant, *Jesus* (London: Rigel, 2004), p. 200.

22. Quoted in McDowell, *Evidence That Demands a Verdict*, vol. 1, p. 193.

Objection No. 6: Jesus Is Not the Only Way to Heaven

1. *Newsweek*/Beliefnet national poll of 1,004 adults, www.beliefnet.com.

2. Lee Weeks, "Teens Not Sure Christianity Is Only Way," *Pulpit Helps* (January 2001).

3. Excerpt from *Back to Bethel* by J. Vernon McGee, quoted in "Thru the Bible Radio" (Pasadena, CA, June 1996).

4. Jerry Adler, "In Search of the Spiritual," *Newsweek*, August 29-September 5, pp. 46-54.

5. Ibid., p. 49.

6. Ravi Zacharias, *Can Man Live Without God* (Nashville, TN: W Publishing Group, 1996).

7. "Heaven: Where Is It? How Do We Get There?" ABC News (December 19, 2005).

Objection No. 7: A Loving God Wouldn't Send People to Hell

1. Greg Garrison, "Heated Debate: Do Hell's Fires Still Burn? Theologians Argue Over Nature, Definition of Bible's Destination for the Wicked," *The Holland Sentinel Archives*, www.hollandsentinel.com.

2. Peter Kreeft and Ron Tacelli, *Handbook of Christian Apologetics* (Downer's Grove, IL: Intervarsity Press, 1994), p. 327.

3. C. S. Lewis, *The Problem of Pain* (New York: MacMillan Publishers, 1962), p. 118.

Objection No. 8: People Are Basically Good

1. "Pregnant Woman Attacked for Her Baby," Associated Press, October 14, 2005.

2. Dorothy Illing and Sid Maher, "Charges Laid Over Old Couple's Murder," news.com.au, January 4, 2006.

3. "Wanted Teenagers Arrested for Gang Rape," *Sun Star,* December 29, 2005.

4. Jeremy McDermott, "Child Mass Murder Suspect Arrested," BBC News Online, January 1, 1999. http://news.bbc.co.uk/1/hi/world/americas/245689.stm (accessed December 2006).

5. "Kuwait Reels as Details of Grisly Murder Surface," *Arab News* (January 29, 2005).

6. Quoted in Thomas Fuller, *The Holy State and the Profane* State (New York: Columbia University Press, 1938).

7. Quoted by Sid Madwed, "Why We Should Read Quotations," www.madwed.com/Quotations.

Objection No. 9: Christians Are All Hypocrites

1. Michael E. Rusten and Sharon Rusten, *When and Where in the Bible and Throughout History* (Wheaton, IL: Tyndale, 2005), pp. 166-167.
2. Samuel P. Huntington, *The Clash Of Civilizations* (New York: Simon & Schuster, 1997), p. 217.
3. Ibid., pp. 256-258.
4. Ibid., p. 293.
5. *Newsweek* (December 24, 2001).
6. Norman Geisler and Frank Turek, *I Don't Have Enough Faith to Be an Atheist* (Wheaton, IL: Crossway Publishers, 2004), p. 296.
7. Hugh R. Trevor-Roper, trans., *Hitler's Table Talk 1941–1944* (New York: Enigma Books, 2002), pp. 118-119.
8. *Nuremberg Trial Proceedings, vol. 2,* The Avalon Project at the Yale Law School, www.yale.edy/lawweb/Avalon/imt/proc/11-21-45.htm.
9. J. E. Persico, *Nuremberg: Infamy on Trial* (New York: Penguin Books, 1994), p. 82.

Objection No. 10: A Merciful God Wouldn't Allow Suffering

1. Lifestyle Information Service, Issue No. 3382 (September 29, 2005).
2. C. S. Lewis, *The Problem of Pain* (San Francisco: HarperSan Francisco, 2001), p. 53.
3. Tom Carter, *2,200 Quotations from the Writings of Charles Spurgeon* (Grand Rapids, MI: Baker Books, 1995), p. 202.
4. Dorothy Sayers, *Christian Letters to a Post-Christian World* (Grand Rapids, MI: William B. Eerdman's Publishing, 1969), p. 14.
5. Quoted by Jon Bos, ed., *Family Magazine* (November/December 2005), p. 7.
6. Lewis, *The Problem of Pain*, p. 93.

Appendix I: "You've Decided to Believe What?!"

1. Josh McDowell and Bob Hostetler, *Beyond Belief to Convictions* (Wheaton, IL: Tyndale Publishers, 2002), pp. 6-7.

2. James W. Sire, *Discipleship of the Mind* (Downers Grove, IL: Intervarsity Press, 1990), pp. 29-30. For more information on Christianity and competing worldviews, I recommend Sire's renowned work *The Universe Next Door* (Downers Grove, IL: Intervarsity Press, 1997).

FURTHER READING

For continued study on apologetics and the
Christian worldview, visit the following:

www.ses.edu
Southern Evangelical Seminary and the Veritas Graduate
School of Religion were founded by apologetics leader
Norman L. Geisler. SES/Veritas offers accredited bachelors,
masters and doctoral level degrees—both residency and dis-
tanced programs—that equip Christian leaders in the biblical
worldview and defense of the faith.

www.wheatstoneacademy.org
Wheatstone Academy offers teens and college students a
weeklong summer program in apologetics training. Wheatstone
Academy features cutting-edge content, exciting seminars and
personal interaction with leading apologists and Christian
thinkers. This unique experience will sharpen the thinking
skills of Christian teens and prompt them to become
all that God intended.

www.beyondbelief.com
This is the website of apologetics leader Josh McDowell.
It features downloadable resources, Josh's travel schedule
and information on how the Beyond Belief campaign
can touch your community for Christ.

For current news on Alex McFarland, scheduling info and more, visit:
www.faithinfocus.org